D1556897

THE LITTLE BOOK FOR BOYS

M. L. STRATTON

Aadamsmedia
AVON, MASSACHUSETTS

Published by
Adams Media, a division of F+W Media, Inc.
57 Littlefield Street, Avon, MA 02322. U.S.A.
www.adamsmedia.com

ISBN 10: 1-4405-2895-0
ISBN 13: 978-1-4405-2895-8
eISBN 10: 1-4405-2988-4
eISBN 13: 978-1-4405-2988-7

Printed by RR Donnelley, Harrisonburg, VA, USA.
10 9 8 7 6 5 4 3 2 1
September 2011

Library of Congress Cataloging-in-Publication Data
is available from the publisher.

This publication is designed to provide accurate and authoritative information with regard
to the subject matter covered. It is sold with the understanding that the publisher is not
engaged in rendering legal, accounting, or other professional advice. If legal advice or
other expert assistance is required, the services of a competent professional person should
be sought.
— From a *Declaration of Principles* jointly adopted by a Committee of the American Bar
Association and a Committee of Publishers and Associations

Recipe for Gingerbread Men is excerpted from *The Everything® Cookies & Brownies Cookbook* by Marye Audet, © 2009 by F+W Media, Inc., ISBN 10: 1605501255, ISBN-13:
978-1605501253.

"Hide and Seek" is excerpted from *Peacock Pie, A Book of Rhymes* by Walter de la Mare,
found at www.gutenberg.org/ebooks/3753.

"A House of Cards" is excerpted from *Sing Song: A Nursery Rhyme Book* by Christina Ros-
setti, London: Macmillan and Co. and New York, 1893.

"Old King Cole," "Georgy Porgy," "Jack Sprat," "Little Jack Horner," "Little Tom
Tucker," "The Cat and the Fiddle," "Pat-a-Cake," "Hickory Dickory Dock," "Humpty Dumpty," "Jack and Jill," "Three Blind Mice," "One, Two, Buckle My Shoe,"
"Wee Willie Winkie," "Simple Simon," "Peter, Peter, Pumpkin Eater," "The Crooked
Sixpence," "Baa, Baa, Black Sheep," "Peter Piper," "Little Boy Blue," "Bedtime,"
and "Come Out to Play" are excerpted from *The Real Mother Goose*, found at www
.gutenberg.org/ebooks/10607.

"Rub-a-Dub" is excerpted from *The Nursery Rhymes of England* by J.O. Halliwell, London
and New York: Frederick Warne and Co., 1886.

This book is available at quantity discounts for bulk purchases.
For information, please call 1-800-289-0963.

DEDICATION

For my boys, Elias and Griffin.
Your spirit, laughter, and wonder make life extraordinary.

ᕙ Acknowledgments ᕗ

Researching and writing this book has been a true joy, and I must begin by wholeheartedly thanking my editor, Andrea, for this wonderful and incredible opportunity. *Thank you.*

And without my amazingly supportive and handsome husband, DBS, I never could have managed such an endeavor. You, I love. My most sincere thanks to my family and my friends for brainstorming with me, for watching my children, for supporting me and encouraging me along the way . . . for everything. I feel so blessed. I can only hope that you, the reader, will enjoy this treasury as much as I've delighted in dreaming it and writing it!

MLS

Matthew 21:16

"If it's half as good as the half we've known, here's Hail! to the rest of the road." —Sheldon Vanauken, *A Severe Mercy*

INTRODUCTION

What are little boys made of?
Frogs and snails
And puppy-dogs' tails,
That's what little boys are made of.

No one can steal your heart faster than your delightful little boy. His is a charm you cannot resist, from his goofy grins and sly smiles to his precious pouts and squeals of delight.

There are the timeless images that you'll cherish as your adorable baby boy grows into a handsome young man: tree forts and tug of war . . . spaceships and superheroes . . . cowboy hats and comic books. Here, in this memorable treasury, you'll find songs, poems, rhymes, and games to share with your son and celebrate the things that make being a little boy so special.

Because being special is what being a little boy is all about!

POEMS

Old King Cole

Old King Cole
Was a merry old soul,
And a merry old soul was he;
He called for his pipe,
And he called for his bowl,
And he called for his
fiddlers three!
And every fiddler, he
had a fine fiddle,
And a very fine fiddle had he.
"Twee tweedle dee, tweedle dee,"
went the fiddlers.
Oh, there's none so rare
As can compare
With King Cole and his
fiddlers three.

Tom, Tom, the Piper's Son

Tom, Tom, the piper's son,
Stole a pig, and away did run;
The pig was eat
And Tom was beat,
And Tom went crying
Down the street.
Tom, Tom, he was a piper's son,
He learned to play
when he was young.

And all the tune that
he could play
Was over the hills and far away;
Over the hills is a great way off.
The wind shall blow
my top-knot off.
Tom with his pipe made
such a noise,
That he pleased both the
girls and boys,
And they all stopped to
hear him play,
'Over the hills and far away.'

Rub-A-Dub

Rub-a-dub-dub
Three men in a tub;
And who do you think they be?
The butcher, the baker,
The candlestick maker;
All scrubbing their way
out to sea.

CRAFT TIME
How to Make Worms in Dirt

Ingredients

- 1 package of instant chocolate pudding, prepared ahead of time (alternatively, you can use purchased single-serving containers of chocolate pudding)
- 1 package of Oreo cookie crumbs (or one package of Oreo cookies, cream filling removed)
- 1 package of gummy worms

1. Decide on what you'd like to serve your dessert in, such as a bowl, cup, or dish. You could use one large serving dish, or make one individual serving per person. If you are using single-serving pudding cups, remove the foil or plastic cover.

2. Spoon the chilled pudding equally into the serving dish(es), leaving room at the top for the crumbs, or "dirt."

3. If you are not using store-bought Oreo cookie wafer crumbs, remove the cream from a package of Oreo cookies with a knife. Place the cookie wafers in a heavy plastic bag and crush them into crumbs with a rolling pin.

4. Top the pudding with the cookie crumbs. Place a few worms on top, stuck into the pudding and poking out through the cookie crumbs to make it look as if the worms are crawling in or out of the ground.

5. Serve and enjoy!

Aladdin and the Wonderful Lamp

here once lived a poor tailor, who had a son called Aladdin, a careless, idle boy who would do nothing but play ball all day long in the streets with little idle boys like himself. This so grieved the father that he died; yet, in spite of his mother's tears and prayers, Aladdin did not mend his ways. One day, when he was playing in the streets as usual, a stranger asked him his age, and if he was not the son of Mustapha the tailor. "I am, sir," replied Aladdin; "but he died a long while ago." On this the stranger, who was a famous African magician, fell on his neck and kissed him, saying, "I am your uncle, and knew you from your likeness to my brother. Go to your mother and tell her I am coming." Aladdin ran home and told his mother of his newly found uncle. "Indeed, child," she said, "your father had a brother, but I always thought he was dead." However, she prepared supper, and bade Aladdin seek his uncle, who came laden with wine and fruit. He presently fell down and kissed the place where Mustapha used to sit, bidding Aladdin's mother not to be surprised at not having seen him before, as he had been forty years out of the country. He then turned to Aladdin, and asked him his trade, at which the boy hung his head, while his mother burst into tears. On learning that Aladdin was idle and would learn no trade, he offered to take a shop for him and stock it with merchandise. Next day he bought Aladdin a fine suit of clothes and took him all over the city, showing him the sights, and brought him home at nightfall to his mother, who was overjoyed to see her son so fine.

The next day the magician led Aladdin into some beautiful gardens a long way outside the city gates. They sat down by a fountain and the magician pulled a cake from his girdle, which he divided between them. They then journeyed onward till they almost reached the mountains. Aladdin was so tired that he begged to go back, but the magician beguiled him with pleasant stories, and led him on in spite of himself. At last they came to two mountains divided by a narrow valley. "We will go no farther," said the false uncle. "I will show you something wonderful; only do you gather up sticks while I kindle a fire." When it was lit the magician threw on it a powder he had about him, at the same time saying some magical words. The earth trembled a little and opened in front of them, disclosing a square flat stone with a brass ring in the middle to raise it by. Aladdin tried to run away, but the magician caught him and gave him a blow that knocked him down. "What have I done, uncle?" he said piteously; whereupon the magician said more kindly: "Fear nothing, but obey me. Beneath this stone lies a treasure which is to be yours, and no one else may touch it, so you must do exactly as I tell you." At the word treasure Aladdin forgot his fears, and grasped the ring as he was told, saying the names of his father and grandfather. The stone came up quite easily, and some steps appeared. "Go down," said the magician; "at the foot of those steps you will find an open door leading into three large halls. Tuck up your gown and go through them without touching anything, or you will die instantly. These halls lead into a garden of fine fruit trees. Walk on until you come to a niche in a terrace where stands a lighted lamp. Pour out the oil it contains, and bring it to me." He drew a ring from his finger and gave it to Aladdin, bidding him prosper.

Aladdin found everything as the magician had said, gathered some fruit off the trees, and, having got the lamp, arrived at the mouth of the cave. The magician cried out in a great hurry: "Make haste and give me the lamp." This Aladdin refused to do until he was out of the cave. The magician flew into a terrible passion, and throwing some more powder on to the fire, he said something, and the stone rolled back into its place.

The magician left Persia for ever, which plainly showed that he was no uncle of Aladdin's, but a cunning magician, who had read in his magic books of a wonderful lamp, which would make him the most powerful man in the world. Though he alone knew where to find it, he could only receive it from the hand of another. He had picked out the foolish Aladdin for this purpose, intending to get the lamp and kill him afterward.

For two days Aladdin remained in the dark, crying and lamenting. At last he clasped his hands in prayer, and in so doing rubbed the ring, which the magician had forgotten to take from him. Immediately an enormous and frightful genie rose out of the earth, saying: "What wouldst thou with me? I am the Slave of the Ring, and will obey thee in all things." Aladdin fearlessly replied: "Deliver me from this place!" whereupon the earth opened, and he found himself outside. As soon as his eyes could bear the light he went home, but fainted on the threshold.

When he came to himself he told his mother what had passed, and showed her the lamp and the fruits he had gathered in the garden, which were, in reality, precious stones. He then asked for some food. "Alas! child," she said, "I have nothing in the house, but I have spun a little cotton and will go and sell it." Aladdin bade her keep her cotton, for he would sell the lamp instead. As it was very dirty she began to rub it, that it might fetch a higher price. Instantly a hideous genie appeared, and asked what she would have. She fainted away, but Aladdin, snatching the lamp, said boldly: "Fetch me something to eat!" The genie returned with a silver bowl, twelve silver plates containing rich meats, two silver cups, and two bottles of wine. Aladdin's mother, when she came to herself, said: "Whence comes this splendid feast?" "Ask not, but eat," replied Aladdin. So they sat at breakfast till it was dinner-time, and Aladdin told his mother about the lamp. She begged him to sell it, and have nothing to do with devils. "No," said Aladdin, "since chance hath made us aware of its virtues, we will use it, and the ring likewise, which I shall always wear on my finger." When they had eaten all the genie had brought, Aladdin sold one of the silver plates, and so on until none were left. He then had recourse to the genie, who gave him another set of plates, and thus they lived for many years.

One day Aladdin heard an order from the Sultan proclaimed that everyone was to stay at home and close his shutters while the Princess, his daughter, went to and from the bath. Aladdin was seized by a desire to see her face, which was very difficult, as she always went veiled. He hid himself behind the door of the bath, and peeped through a chink. The Princess lifted her veil as she went in, and looked so beautiful that Aladdin fell in love with her at first sight. He went home so changed that his mother was frightened. He told her he loved the Princess so deeply that he could not live without her, and meant to ask her in marriage of her father. His mother, on hearing this, burst out laughing, but Aladdin at last prevailed upon her to go before the Sultan and carry his request.

She fetched a napkin and laid in it the magic fruits from the enchanted garden, which sparkled and shone like the most beautiful jewels. She took these with her to please the Sultan, and set out, trusting in the lamp. The Grand Vizier and the lords of council had just gone in as she entered the hall and placed herself in front of the Sultan. He, however, took no notice of her. She went every day for a week, and stood in the same place. When the council broke up on the sixth day the Sultan said to his Vizier: "I see a certain woman in the audience-chamber every day carrying something in a napkin. Call her next time, that I may find out what she wants." Next day, at a sign from the Vizier, she went up to the foot of the throne and remained kneeling till the Sultan said to her: "Rise, good woman, and tell me what you want." She hesitated, so the Sultan sent away all but the Vizier, and bade her speak frankly, promising to forgive her beforehand for anything she might say. She then told him of her son's violent love for the Princess. "I prayed him to forget her," she said, "but in vain; he threatened to do some desperate deed if I refused to go and ask your Majesty for the hand of the Princess. Now I pray you to forgive not me alone, but my son Aladdin." The Sultan asked her kindly what she had in the napkin, whereupon she unfolded the jewels and presented them. He was thunderstruck, and turning to the Vizier said: "What sayest thou? Ought I not to bestow the Princess on one who values her at such a price?" The Vizier, who wanted her for his own son, begged the Sultan to withhold her for three months, in the course of which he hoped his son would contrive to make him a richer present. The Sultan granted this, and told Aladdin's mother that, though he consented to the marriage, she must not appear before him again for three months.

Aladdin waited patiently for nearly three months, but after two had elapsed his mother, going into the city to buy oil, found every one rejoicing, and asked what was going on. "Do you not know," was the answer, "that the son of the Grand Vizier is to marry the Sultan's daughter to-night?" Breathless, she ran and told Aladdin, who was overwhelmed at first, but presently bethought him of the lamp. He rubbed it, and the genie appeared, saying, "What is thy will?" Aladdin replied: "The Sultan, as thou knowest, has broken his promise to me, and the Vizier's son is to have the Princess. My command is that to-night you bring hither the bride and bridegroom." "Master, I obey," said the genie. Aladdin then went to his chamber, where, sure enough, at midnight the genie transported the bed containing the Vizier's son and the Princess. "Take this new-married man," he said, "and put him outside in the cold, and return at daybreak." Whereupon the genie took the Vizier's son out of bed, leaving Aladdin with the Princess. "Fear nothing," Aladdin said to her; "you are my wife, promised to me by your unjust father, and no harm shall come to you." The Princess was too frightened to speak, and passed the most miserable night of her life, while Aladdin lay down beside her and slept soundly. At the appointed hour the genie fetched in the shivering bridegroom, laid him in his place, and transported the bed back to the palace.

Presently the Sultan came to wish his daughter good morning. The unhappy Vizier's son jumped up and hid himself, while the Princess would not say a word, and was very sorrowful. The Sultan sent her mother to her, who said: "How comes it, child, that you will not speak to your father? What has happened?" The Princess sighed deeply, and at last told her mother how, during the night, the bed had been carried into some strange house, and what had passed there. Her mother did not believe her in the least, but bade her rise and consider it an idle dream.

The following night exactly the same thing happened, and next morning, on the Princess's refusal to speak, the Sultan threatened to cut off her head. She then confessed all, bidding him to ask the Vizier's son if it were not so. The Sultan told the Vizier to ask his son, who owned the truth, adding that, dearly as he loved the Princess, he had rather die than go through another such fearful night, and wished to be separated from her. His wish was granted, and there was an end to feasting and rejoicing.

When the three months were over, Aladdin sent his mother to remind the Sultan of his promise. She stood in the same place as before, and the Sultan, who had forgotten Aladdin, at once remembered him, and sent for her. On seeing her poverty the Sultan felt less inclined than ever to keep his word, and asked his Vizier's advice, who counseled him to set so high a value on the Princess that no man living could come up to it. The Sultan then turned to Aladdin's mother, saying: "Good woman, a Sultan must remember his promises, and I will remember mine, but your son must first send me forty basins of gold brimful of jewels, carried by forty black slaves, led by as many white ones, splendidly dressed. Tell him that I await his answer." The mother of Aladdin bowed low and went home, thinking all was lost. She gave Aladdin the message, adding: "He may wait long enough for your answer!" "Not so long, mother, as you think," her son replied. "I would do a great deal more than that for the Princess." He summoned the genie, and in a few moments the eighty slaves arrived, and filled up the small house and garden. Aladdin made them set out to the palace, two and two, followed by his mother. They were so richly dressed, with such splendid jewels in their girdles, that everyone crowded to see them and the basins of gold they carried on their heads.

They entered the palace, and, after kneeling before the Sultan, stood in a half-circle round the throne with their arms crossed, while Aladdin's mother presented them to the Sultan. He hesitated no longer, but said: "Good woman, return and tell your son that I wait for him with open arms." She lost no time in telling Aladdin, bidding him make haste. But Aladdin first called the genie. "I want a scented bath," he said, "a richly embroidered habit, a horse surpassing the Sultan's, and twenty slaves to attend me. Besides this, six slaves, beautifully dressed, to wait on my mother; and lastly, ten thousand pieces of gold in ten purses." No sooner said than done. Aladdin mounted his horse and passed through the streets, the slaves strewing gold as they went. Those who had played with him in his childhood knew him not, he had grown so handsome. When the Sultan saw him he came down from his throne, embraced him, and led him into a hall where a feast was spread, intending to marry him to the Princess that very day. But Aladdin refused, saying, "I must build a palace fit for her," and took his leave. Once home, he said to the genie: "Build me a palace of the finest marble, set with jasper, agate, and other precious stones. In the middle you shall build me a large hall with a dome, its four walls of massy gold and silver, each having six windows, whose lattices, all except one which is to be left unfinished, must be set with diamonds and rubies. There must be stables and horses and grooms and slaves; go and see about it!"

The palace was finished by the next day, and the genie carried him there and showed him all his orders faithfully carried out, even to the laying of a velvet carpet from Aladdin's palace to the Sultan's. Aladdin's mother then dressed herself carefully, and walked to the palace with her slaves, while he followed her on horseback. The Sultan sent musicians with trumpets and cymbals to meet them, so that the air resounded with music and cheers. She was taken to the Princess, who saluted her and treated her with great honor. At night the Princess said goodbye to her father, and set out on the carpet for Aladdin's palace, with his mother at her side, and followed by the hundred slaves. She was charmed at the sight of Aladdin, who ran to receive her. "Princess," he said, "blame your beauty for my boldness if I have displeased you." She told him that, having seen him, she willingly obeyed her father in this matter.

After the wedding had taken place Aladdin led her into the hall, where a feast was spread, and she supped with him, after which they danced till midnight. Next day Aladdin invited the Sultan to see the palace. On entering the hall with the four-and-twenty windows, with their rubies, diamonds, and emeralds, he cried: "It is a world's wonder! There is only one thing that surprises me. Was it by accident that one window was left unfinished?" "No, sir, by design," returned Aladdin. "I wished your Majesty to have the glory of finishing this palace." The Sultan was pleased, and sent for the best jewelers in the city. He showed them the unfinished window, and bade them fit it up like the others. "Sir," replied their spokesman, "we cannot find jewels enough." The Sultan had his own fetched, which they soon used, but to no purpose, for in a month's time the work was not half done. Aladdin, knowing that their task was vain, bade them undo their work and carry the jewels back, and the genie finished the window at his command. The Sultan was surprised to receive his jewels again, and visited Aladdin, who showed him the window finished. The Sultan embraced him, the envious Vizier meanwhile hinting that it was the work of enchantment.

Aladdin had won the hearts of the people by his gentle bearing. He was made captain of the Sultan's armies, and won several battles for him, but remained modest and courteous as before, and lived thus in peace and content for several years.

But far away in Africa the magician remembered Aladdin, and by his magic arts discovered that Aladdin, instead of perishing miserably in the cave, had escaped, and had married a princess, with whom he was living in great honor and wealth. He knew that the poor tailor's son could only have accomplished this by means of the lamp, and traveled night and day until he reached the capital of China, bent on Aladdin's ruin. As he passed through the town he heard people talking everywhere about a marvelous palace. "Forgive my ignorance," he asked, "what is this palace you speak of?" "Have you not heard of Prince Aladdin's palace," was the reply, "the greatest wonder of the world? I will direct you if you have a mind to see it." The magician thanked him who spoke, and having seen the palace, knew that it had been raised by the Genie of the Lamp, and became half mad with rage. He determined to get hold of the lamp, and again plunge Aladdin into the deepest poverty.

Unluckily, Aladdin had gone a-hunting for eight days, which gave the magician plenty of time. He bought a dozen copper lamps, put them into a basket, and went to the palace, crying: "New lamps for old!" followed by a jeering crowd. The Princess, sitting in the hall of four-and-twenty windows, sent a slave to find out what the noise was about, who came back laughing, so that the Princess scolded her. "Madam," replied the slave, "who can help laughing to see an old fool offering to exchange fine new lamps for old ones?" Another slave, hearing this, said: "There is an old one on the cornice there which he can have." Now this was the magic lamp, which Aladdin had left there, as he could not take it out hunting with him. The Princess, not knowing its value, laughingly bade the slave take it and make the exchange. She went and said to the magician: "Give me a new lamp for this." He snatched it and bade the slave take her choice, amid the jeers of the crowd. Little he cared, but left off crying his lamps, and went out of the city gates to a lonely place, where he remained till nightfall, when he pulled out the lamp and rubbed it. The genie appeared, and at the magician's command carried him, together with the palace and the Princess in it, to a lonely place in Africa.

Next morning the Sultan looked out of the window toward Aladdin's palace and rubbed his eyes, for it was gone. He sent for the Vizier and asked what had become of the palace. The Vizier looked out too, and was lost in astonishment. He again put it down to enchantment, and this time the Sultan believed him, and sent thirty men on horseback to fetch Aladdin in chains. They met him riding home, bound him, and forced him to go with them on foot. The people, however, who loved him, followed, armed, to see that he came to no harm. He was carried before the Sultan, who ordered the executioner to cut off his head. The executioner made Aladdin kneel down, bandaged his eyes, and raised his scimitar to strike. At that instant the Vizier, who saw that the crowd had forced their way into the courtyard and were scaling the walls to rescue Aladdin, called to the executioner to stay his hand. The people, indeed, looked so threatening that the Sultan gave way and ordered Aladdin to be unbound, and pardoned him in the sight of the crowd. Aladdin now begged to know what he had done. "False wretch!" said the Sultan, "come thither," and showed him from the window the place where his palace had stood. Aladdin was so amazed that he could not say a word. "Where is my palace and my daughter?" demanded the Sultan. "For the first I am not so deeply concerned, but my daughter I must have, and you must find her or lose your head." Aladdin begged for forty days in which to find her, promising, if he failed, to return and suffer death at the Sultan's pleasure. His prayer was granted, and he went forth sadly from the Sultan's presence.

For three days he wandered about like a madman, asking everyone what had become of his palace, but they only laughed and pitied him. He came to the banks of a river, and knelt down to say his prayers before throwing himself in. In so doing he rubbed the magic ring he still wore. The genie he had seen in the cave appeared, and asked his will. "Save my life, genie," said Aladdin, "bring my palace back." "That is not in my power," said the genie; "I am only the Slave of the Ring; you must ask him of the lamp." "Even so," said Aladdin, "but thou canst take me to the palace, and set me down under my dear wife's window." He at once found himself in Africa, under the window of the Princess, and fell asleep out of sheer weariness.

He was awakened by the singing of the birds, and his heart was lighter. He saw plainly that all his misfortunes were owing to the loss of the lamp, and vainly wondered who had robbed him of it.

That morning the Princess rose earlier than she had done since she had been carried into Africa by the magician, whose company she was forced to endure once a day. She, however, treated him so harshly that he dared not live there altogether. As she was dressing, one of her women looked out and saw Aladdin. The Princess ran and opened the window, and at the noise she made Aladdin looked up. She called to him to come to her, and great was the joy of these lovers at seeing each other again. After he had kissed her Aladdin said: "I beg of you, Princess, in God's name, before we speak of anything else, for your own sake and mine, tell me that has become of an old lamp I left on the cornice in the hall of four-and-twenty windows, when I went a-hunting." "Alas!" she said, "I am the innocent cause of our sorrows," and told him of the exchange of the lamp. "Now I know," cried Aladdin, "that we have to thank the African magician for this! Where is the lamp?" "He carries it about with him," said the Princess. "I know, for he pulled it out of his breast to show me. He wishes me to break my faith with you and marry him, saying that you were beheaded by my father's command. He is forever speaking ill of you but I only reply by my tears. If I persist, I doubt not but he will use violence." Aladdin comforted her, and left her for a while. He changed clothes with the first person he met in the town, and having bought a certain powder, returned to the Princess, who let him in by a little side door.

"Put on your most beautiful dress," he said to her "and receive the magician with smiles, leading him to believe that you have forgotten me. Invite him to sup with you, and say you wish to taste the wine of his country. He will go for some and while he is gone I will tell you what to do." She listened carefully to Aladdin and when he left she arrayed herself gaily for the first time since she left China. She put on a girdle and head-dress of diamonds, and, seeing in a glass that she was more beautiful than ever, received the magician, saying, to his great amazement: "I have made up my mind that Aladdin is dead, and that all my tears will not bring him back to me, so I am resolved to mourn no more, and have therefore invited you to sup with me; but I am tired of the wines of China, and would fain taste those of Africa."

The magician flew to his cellar, and the Princess put the powder Aladdin had given her in her cup. When he returned she asked him to drink her health in the wine of Africa, handing him her cup in exchange for his, as a sign she was reconciled to him. Before drinking the magician made her a speech in praise of her beauty, but the Princess cut him short, saying: "Let us drink first, and you shall say what you will afterward." She set her cup to her lips and kept it there, while the magician drained his to the dregs and fell back lifeless. The Princess then opened the door to Aladdin, and flung her arms round his neck; but Aladdin put her away, bidding her leave him, as he had more to do. He then went to the dead magician, took the lamp out of his vest, and bade the genie carry the palace and all in it back to China. This was done, and the Princess in her chamber only felt two little shocks, and little thought she was at home again.

The Sultan, who was sitting in his closet, mourning for his lost daughter, happened to look up, and rubbed his eyes, for there stood the palace as before! He hastened thither, and Aladdin received him in the hall of the four-and-twenty windows, with the Princess at his side. Aladdin told him what had happened, and showed him the dead body of the magician, that he might believe. A ten days' feast was proclaimed, and it seemed as if Aladdin might now live the rest of his life in peace; but it was not to be.

The African magician had a younger brother, who was, if possible, more wicked and more cunning than himself. He traveled to China to avenge his brother's death, and went to visit a pious woman called Fatima, thinking she might be of use to him. He entered her cell and clapped a dagger to her breast, telling her to rise and do his bidding on pain of death. He changed clothes with her, colored his face like hers, put on her veil, and murdered her, that she might tell no tales. Then he went toward the palace of Aladdin, and all the people, thinking he was the holy woman, gathered round him, kissing his hands and begging his blessing. When he got to the palace there was such a noise going on round him that the Princess bade her slave look out of the window and ask what was the matter. The slave said it was the holy woman, curing people by her touch of their ailments, whereupon the Princess, who had long desired to see Fatima, sent for her. On coming to the Princess the magician offered up a prayer for her health and prosperity. When he had done the Princess made him sit by her, and begged him to stay with her always. The false Fatima, who wished for nothing better, consented, but kept his veil down for fear of discovery. The Princess showed him the hall, and asked him what he thought of it. "It is truly beautiful," said the false

Fatima. "In my mind it wants but one thing." "And what is that?" said the Princess. "If only a roc's egg," replied he, "were hung up from the middle of this dome, it would be the wonder of the world."

After this the Princess could think of nothing but the roc's egg, and when Aladdin returned from hunting he found her in a very ill humor. He begged to know what was amiss, and she told him that all her pleasure in the hall was spoiled for the want of a roc's egg hanging from the dome. "If that is all," replied Aladdin, "you shall soon be happy." He left her and rubbed the lamp, and when the genie appeared commanded him to bring a roc's egg. The genie gave such a loud and terrible shriek that the hall shook. "Wretch!" he cried, "is it not enough that I have done everything for you, but you must command me to bring my master and hang him up in the midst of this dome? You and your wife and your palace deserve to be burnt to ashes, but that this request does not come from you, but from the brother of the African magician, whom you destroyed. He is now in your palace disguised as the holy woman—whom he murdered. He it was who put that wish into your wife's head. Take care of yourself, for he means to kill you." So saying, the genie disappeared.

Aladdin went back to the Princess, saying his head ached, and requesting that the holy Fatima should be fetched to lay her hands on it. But when the magician came near, Aladdin, seizing his dagger, pierced him to the heart. "What have you done?" cried the Princess. "You have killed the holy woman!" "Not so," replied Aladdin, "but a wicked magician," and told her of how she had been deceived.

After this Aladdin and his wife lived in peace. He succeeded the Sultan when he died, and reigned for many years, leaving behind him a long line of kings.

A boy is a magical creature——you can lock him out of your workshop, but you can't lock him out of your heart.

——ALLAN BECK

THIS OLD MAN

This old man, he played one

He played knick-knack on my thumb

With a knick-knack patty-whack, give a dog a bone

This old man came rolling home

This old man, he played two

He played knick-knack on my shoe

With a knick-knack patty-whack, give a dog a bone

This old man came rolling home

This old man, he played three

He played knick-knack on my knee

With a knick-knack patty-whack, give a dog a bone

This old man came rolling home

This old man, he played four

He played knick-knack on my door

With a knick-knack patty-whack, give a dog a bone

This old man came rolling home

This old man, he played five

He played knick-knack on my hive

With a knick-knack patty-whack, give a dog a bone

This old man came rolling home

This old man, he played six

He played knick-knack on my sticks

With a knick-knack patty-whack, give a dog a bone

This old man came rolling home

This old man, he played seven

He played knick-knack up in heaven

With a knick-knack patty-whack, give a dog a bone

This old man came rolling home

This old man, he played eight

He played knick-knack on my gate

With a knick-knack patty-whack, give a dog a bone

This old man came rolling home

This old man, he played nine

He played knick-knack on my spine

With a knick-knack patty-whack, give a dog a bone

This old man came rolling home

This old man, he played ten

He played knick-knack once again

With a knick-knack patty-whack, give a dog a bone

This old man came rolling home

CRAFT TIME
Stone Soup

Ingredients
YIELDS 6–8 SERVINGS

- 1 tablespoon butter
- 1 pound stewing beef, cut into small pieces
- 1 teaspoon salt
- ½ teaspoon pepper
- 2 small onions, diced
- 6 cups water
- 3 beef bouillon cubes
- 1 stone (not too small and cleaned well!)
- 1 cabbage, chopped
- 4 carrots, diced
- 4–5 red potatoes, diced
- 1 tablespoon sage
- 1 tablespoon parsley

1. Heat butter in a deep stockpot or soup pot and season the beef with salt and pepper.

2. Brown the beef and the onion in the butter for about five minutes.

3. Add water, bouillon cubes, and the stone.

4. Simmer over medium heat for an hour.

5. After the soup simmers, add the cabbage, carrots, and potatoes to the pot.

6. Season with sage and parsley and simmer on low heat for one more hour.

You are worried about seeing him spend his early years in doing nothing. What! Is it nothing to be happy? Nothing to skip, play, and run around all day long? Never in his life will he be so busy again.

——JEAN-JACQUES ROUSSEAU,
EMILE, 1762

POEMS

Georgy Porgy

Georgy Porgy, pudding and pie,
Kissed the girls and made them
cry
When the boys came out to play,
Georgy Porgy ran away.

Little Tom Tucker

Little Tom Tucker
Sings for his supper,
What shall he eat?
White bread and butter.
How will he cut it
Without e'er a knife?
How will he be married
Without e'er a wife?

The Cat and the Fiddle

Hey, diddle, diddle!
The cat and the fiddle,
The cow jumped over the moon;
The little dog laughed
To see such sport,
And the dish ran away with
the spoon.

Jack Sprat

Jack Sprat
Could eat no fat,
His wife could eat no lean;
And so,
Betwixt them both,
They licked the platter clean

Little Jack Horner

Little Jack Horner
Sat in the corner,
Eating of Christmas pie:
He put in his thumb,
And pulled out a plum,
And said, "What a good
boy am I!"

Frere Jacques

Frere Jacques,
Frere Jacques,
Dormez vous?
Dormez vous?
Sonnez les matines,
Sonnez les matines.
Ding Ding Dong,
Ding Ding Dong.

SONGS THAT CELEBRATE YOUR SON

- "Beautiful Boy"
  by John Lennon
- "Just the Two of Us"
  by Will Smith
- "I See Me"
  by Travis Tritt
- "A Song for Mama"
  by Boyz II Men
- "Watching You"
  by Rodney Atkins
- "My Wish"
  by Rascal Flatts
- "The Riddle"
  by Five for Fighting
- "Mammas Don't Let Your Babies Grow Up to Be Cowboys"
  by Waylon Jennings & Willie Nelson
- "Simple Man"
  by Lynyrd Skynyrd
- "He Gets That from Me"
  by Reba McEntire
- "Sons Of"
  by Judy Collins
- "Beautiful Boy"
  by Celine Dion

CLASSIC FATHER-SON MOVIES

- *Star Wars*
- *Mrs. Doubtfire*
- *The Lion King*
- *Pinocchio*
- *Chitty Chitty Bang Bang*
- *Finding Nemo*
- *How to Train Your Dragon*
- *Rudy*
- *Like Father, Like Son*
- *Indiana Jones and the Last Crusade*
- *Big Fish*

CRAFT TIME
Gingerbread Men

This is very soft dough; be sure to keep it well chilled and allow plenty of room on the cookie sheet for the dough to spread.

Ingredients
YIELDS 36 COOKIES

- 1 cup packed dark brown sugar
- ¾ cup sugar
- ½ cup vegetable shortening
- 2 eggs
- ¼ cup molasses
- ½ teaspoon vanilla
- 2 cups all-purpose flour
- 1 teaspoon baking soda
- 1 teaspoon baking powder
- 1½ teaspoons ginger
- 1 teaspoon salt
- 1 teaspoon cinnamon
- ¼ teaspoon white pepper or cayenne
- ¼ teaspoon ground cloves
- Raw sugar for sprinkling

1. Cream together sugars and shortening until fluffy. Add eggs, molasses, and vanilla.

2. Whisk together dry ingredients until smooth; add to shortening mixture. Blend well. Chill overnight.

3. Preheat oven to 300°F. Place parchment on cookie sheets.

4. Roll dough ⅛" thick on heavily floured surface. Cut with floured cookie cutters and transfer to parchment. Sprinkle with raw sugar if desired.

5. Bake 15–18 minutes, or until done.

BOOKS TO COLLECT FOR YOUR SON

The stories we grow up reading shape our lives, and creating a library of books is one of the greatest gifts you could give your child. Here is a list of some of the most treasured classics to help start your son's very own collection.

The Tale of Peter Rabbit by Beatrix Potter
Jumanji by Chris Van Allsburg
Grimm's Fairy Tales by Jacob and Wilhelm Grimm
Winnie-the-Pooh by A. A. Milne
The Wind in the Willows by Kenneth Grahame
Stuart Little by E. B. White
Pinocchio by Carlo Collodi
The Chronicles of Narnia by C.S. Lewis
The Borrowers by Mary Norton
The Wonderful Wizard of Oz by L. Frank Baum
The Incredible Journey by Sheila Burnford
The Hardy Boys books by Franklin W. Dixon
Adventures of Huckleberry Finn by Mark Twain
The Swiss Family Robinson by Johann David Wyss
Oliver Twist by Charles Dickens
Around the World in 80 Days by Jules Verne
The Call of the Wild by Jack London
The Adventures of Sherlock Holmes by Sir Arthur Conan Doyle
Robinson Crusoe by Daniel Defoe
Lord of the Flies by William Golding
Gulliver's Travels by Jonathan Swift
Moby Dick by Herman Melville

A boy is Truth with dirt on its face, Beauty with a cut on its finger, Wisdom with bubble gum in its hair, and the Hope of the future with a frog in its pocket.

——ALAN MARSHALL BECK

Blue Beard

BY CHARLES PERRAULT

 here was a man who had fine houses, both in town and country, a deal of silver and gold plate, embroidered furniture, and coaches gilded all over with gold. But this man had the misfortune to have a blue beard, which made him so frightfully ugly, that all the women and girls ran away from him.

One of his neighbors, a lady of quality, had two daughters who were perfect beauties. He desired of her one of them in marriage, leaving to her the choice which of the two she would bestow upon him. They would neither of them have him, and each made the other welcome of him, being not able to bear the thought of marrying a man who had a blue beard. And what besides gave them disgust and aversion, was his having already been married to several wives, and nobody ever knew what became of them.

Blue Beard, to engage their affection, took them, with the lady their mother, and three or four ladies of their acquaintance, with other young people of the neighborhood, to one of his country seats, where they stayed a whole week. There was nothing then to be seen but parties of pleasure, hunting, fishing, dancing, mirth, and feasting. Nobody went to bed, but all passed the night in playing tricks upon each other. In short, every thing succeeded so well, that the youngest daughter began to think the master of the house not to have a beard so very blue, and that he was a mighty civil gentleman. As soon as they returned home, the marriage was concluded.

About a month afterwards Blue Beard told his wife that he was obliged to take a country journey for six weeks at least, about affairs of very great consequence, desiring her to divert herself in his absence, to send for her friends and acquaintances, to carry them into the country, if she pleased, and to make good cheer wherever she was.

"Here," said he, "are the keys of the two great wardrobes, wherein I have my best furniture; these are of my silver and gold plate, which is not every day in use; these open my strong boxes, which hold my money, both gold and silver; these my caskets of jewels; and this is the master-key to all my apartments. But for this little one here, it is the key of the closet at the end of the great gallery on the ground floor. Open them all; go into all and every one of them; except that little closet which I forbid you, and forbid it in such a manner that, if you happen to open it, there will be no bounds to my just anger and resentment."

She promised to observe, very exactly, whatever he had ordered; when he, after having embraced her, got into his coach and proceeded on his journey.

Her neighbors and good friends did not stay to be sent for by the newmarried lady, so great was their impatience to see all the rich furniture of her house, not daring to come while her husband was there, because of his blue beard which frightened them. They ran through all the rooms, closets, and wardrobes, which were all so rich and fine, that they seemed to surpass one another.

After that, they went up into the two great rooms, where were the best and richest furniture; they could not sufficiently admire the number and beauty of the tapestry, beds, couches, cabinets, stands, tables, and looking-glasses in which you might see yourself from head to foot; some of them were framed with glass, others with silver, plain and gilded, the finest and most magnificent which were ever seen. They ceased not to extol and envy the happiness of their friend, who in the mean time no way diverted herself in looking upon all these rich things, because of the impatience she had to go and open the closet of the ground floor. She was so much pressed by her curiosity, that, without considering that it was very uncivil to leave her company, she went down a little back staircase, and with such excessive haste, that she had twice or thrice like to have broken her neck.

Being come to the closet door, she made a stop for some time, thinking upon her husband's orders, and considering what unhappiness might attend her if she was disobedient; but the temptation was so strong she could not overcome it. She took then the little key, and opened it trembling; but could not at first see any thing plainly, because the windows were shut. After some moments she began to perceive that the floor was all covered over with clotted blood, in which were reflected the bodies of several dead women ranged against the walls: these were all the wives whom Blue Beard had married and murdered one after another. She was like to have died for fear, and the key, which she pulled out of the lock, fell out of her hand.

After having somewhat recovered her senses, she took up the key, locked the door, and went up stairs into her chamber to recover herself; but she could not, so much was she frightened. Having observed that the key of the closet was stained with blood, she tried two or three times to wipe it off, but the blood would not come off; in vain did she wash it, and even rub it with soap and sand, the blood still remained, for the key was a Fairy, and she could never make it quite clean; when the blood was gone off from one side, it came again on the other.

Blue Beard returned from his journey the same evening, and said he had received letters upon the road, informing him that the affair he went about was ended to his advantage. His wife did all she could to convince him she was extremely glad of his speedy return. Next morning he asked her for the keys, which she gave him, but with such a trembling hand, that he easily guessed what had happened.

"What," said he, "is not the key of my closet among the rest?"

"I must certainly," answered she, "have left it above upon the table."

"Fail not," said Blue Beard, "to bring it me presently."

After putting him off several times, she was forced to bring him the key. Blue Beard, having very attentively considered it, said to his wife:

"How comes this blood upon the key?"

"I do not know," cried the poor woman, paler than death.

"You do not know," replied Blue Beard; "I very well know, you were resolved to go into the closet, were you not? Mighty well, Madam; you shall go in, and take your place among the ladies you saw there."

Upon this she threw herself at her husband's feet, and begged his pardon with all the signs of a true repentance for her disobedience. She would have melted a rock, so beautiful and sorrowful was she; but Blue Beard had a heart harder than any rock.

"You must die, Madam," said he, "and that presently."

"Since I must die," answered she, looking upon him with her eyes all bathed in tears, "give me some little time to say my prayers."

"I give you," replied Blue Beard, "half a quarter of an hour, but not one moment more."

When she was alone, she called out to her sister, and said to her:

"Sister Anne" (for that was her name), "go up I beg you, upon the top of the tower, and look if my brothers are not coming; they promised me that they would come today, and if you see them, give them a sign to make haste."

Her sister Anne went up upon the top of the tower, and the poor afflicted wife cried out from time to time, "Anne, sister Anne, do you see any one coming?"

And sister Anne said:

"I see nothing but the sun, which makes a dust, and the grass growing green."

In the meanwhile Blue Beard, holding a great scimitar in his hand, cried out as loud as he could bawl to his wife:

"Come down instantly, or I shall come up to you."

"One moment longer, if you please," said his wife, and then she cried out very softly:

"Anne, sister Anne, dost thou see anybody coming?"

And sister Anne answered:

"I see nothing but the sun, which makes a dust, and the grass growing green."

"Come down quickly," cried Blue Beard, "or I will come up to you."

"I am coming," answered his wife; and then she cried:

"Anne, sister Anne, dost thou see anyone coming?"

"I see," replied sister Anne, "a great dust that comes this way."

"Are they my brothers?"

"Alas! no, my dear sister, I see a flock of sheep."

"Will you not come down?" cried Blue Beard.

"One moment longer," said his wife, and then she cried out:

"Anne, sister Anne, dost thou see nobody coming?"

"I see," said she, "two horsemen coming, but they are yet a great way off."

"God be praised," she cried presently, "they are my brothers; I am beckoning to them, as well as I can, for them to make haste."

Then Blue Beard bawled out so loud, that he made the whole house tremble. The distressed wife came down, and threw herself at his feet, all in tears, with her hair about her shoulders.

"Nought will avail," said Blue Beard, "you must die"; then, taking hold of her hair with one hand, and lifting up his scimitar with the other, he was going to take off her head.

The poor lady turning about to him, and looking at him with dying eyes, desired him to afford her one little moment to recollect herself.

"No, no," said he, "recommend thyself to God," and was just ready to strike.

At this very instant there was such a loud knocking at the gate, that Blue Beard made a sudden stop. The gate was opened, and presently entered two horsemen, who drawing their swords, ran directly to Blue Beard. He knew them to be his wife's brothers, one a dragoon, the other a musketeer; so that he ran away immediately to save himself; but the two brothers pursued so close, that they overtook him before he could get to the steps of the porch, when they ran their swords through his body and left him dead. The poor wife was almost as dead as her husband, and had not strength enough to rise and welcome her brothers.

Blue Beard had no heirs, and so his wife became mistress of all his estate. She made use of one part of it to marry her sister Anne to a young gentleman who had loved her a long while; another part to buy captains' commissions for her brothers; and the rest to marry herself to a very worthy gentleman, who made her forget the ill time she had passed with Blue Beard.

CRAFT TIME
How to Make Slime

What You'll Need:

- ½ cup warm water
- ½ cup clear or white Elmer's glue (about one 4-ounce bottle)
- Food coloring (optional)
- 2 teaspoons borax (laundry booster)
- 1 cup warm water

1. Mix the ½ cup of warm water and glue in one bowl (if you'd like a colored slime, add food coloring to the mixture at this point).

2. In another bowl, mix borax together with one cup of warm water.

3. Pour the glue mixture into the borax mixture and use your hands to combine the two.

4. Now you're ready to play!

Tom Thumb

BY THE BROTHERS GRIMM

 poor woodman sat in his cottage one night, smoking his pipe by the fireside, while his wife sat by his side spinning. "How lonely it is, wife," said he, as he puffed out a long curl of smoke, "for you and me to sit here by ourselves, without any children to play about and amuse us while other people seem so happy and merry with their children!" "What you say is very true," said the wife, sighing, and turning round her wheel; "how happy should I be if I had but one child! If it were ever so small—nay, if it were no bigger than my thumb—I should be very happy, and love it dearly." Now—odd as you may think it—it came to pass that this good woman's wish was fulfilled, just in the very way she had wished it; for, not long afterwards, she had a little boy, who was quite healthy and strong, but was not much bigger than my thumb. So they said, "Well, we cannot say we have not got what we wished for, and, little as he is, we will love him dearly." And they called him Thomas Thumb.

They gave him plenty of food, yet for all they could do he never grew bigger, but kept just the same size as he had been when he was born. Still, his eyes were sharp and sparkling, and he soon showed himself to be a clever little fellow, who always knew well what he was about.

One day, as the woodman was getting ready to go into the wood to cut fuel, he said, "I wish I had someone to bring the cart after me, for I want to make haste." "Oh, father," cried Tom, "I will take care of that; the cart shall be in the wood by the time you want it." Then the woodman laughed, and said, "How can that be? you cannot reach up to the horse's bridle." "Never mind that, father," said

Tom; "if my mother will only harness the horse, I will get into his ear and tell him which way to go." "Well," said the father, "we will try for once."

When the time came the mother harnessed the horse to the cart, and put Tom into his ear; and as he sat there the little man told the beast how to go, crying out, "Go on!" and "Stop!" as he wanted: and thus the horse went on just as well as if the woodman had driven it himself into the wood. It happened that as the horse was going a little too fast, and Tom was calling out, "Gently! gently!" two strangers came up. "What an odd thing that is!" said one: "there is a cart going along, and I hear a carter talking to the horse, but yet I can see no one." "That is queer, indeed," said the other; "let us follow the cart, and see where it goes." So they went on into the wood, till at last they came to the place where the woodman was. Then Tom Thumb, seeing his father, cried out, "See, father, here I am with the cart, all right and safe! now take me down!" So his father took hold of the horse with one hand, and with the other took his son out of the horse's ear, and put him down upon a straw, where he sat as merry as you please.

The two strangers were all this time looking on, and did not know what to say for wonder. At last one took the other aside, and said, "That little urchin will make our fortune, if we can get him, and carry him about from town to town as a show; we must buy him." So they went up to the woodman, and asked him what he would take for the little man. "He will be better off," said they, "with us than with you." "I won't sell him at all," said the father; "my own flesh and blood is dearer to me than all the silver and gold in the world." But Tom, hearing of the bargain they wanted to make, crept up his father's coat to his shoulder and whispered in his ear, "Take the money, father, and let them have me; I'll soon come back to you."

So the woodman at last said he would sell Tom to the strangers for a large piece of gold, and they paid the price. "Where would you like to sit?" said one of them. "Oh, put me on the rim of your hat; that will be a nice gallery for me; I can walk about there and see the country as we go along." So they did as he wished; and when Tom had taken leave of his father they took him away with them.

They journeyed on till it began to be dusky, and then the little man said, "Let me get down, I'm tired." So the man took off his hat, and put him down on a clod of earth, in a ploughed field by the side of the road. But Tom ran about amongst the furrows, and at last slipped into an old mouse-hole. "Good night, my masters!" said he, "I'm off! mind and look sharp after me the next time." Then they ran at once to the place, and poked the ends of their sticks into the mouse-hole, but all in vain; Tom only crawled farther and farther in; and at last it became quite dark, so that they were forced to go their way without their prize, as sulky as could be.

When Tom found they were gone, he came out of his hiding-place. "What dangerous walking it is," said he, "in this ploughed field! If I were to fall from one of these great clods, I should undoubtedly break my neck." At last, by good luck, he found a large empty snail-shell. "This is lucky," said he, "I can sleep here very well"; and in he crept.

Just as he was falling asleep, he heard two men passing by, chatting together; and one said to the other, "How can we rob that rich parson's house of his silver and gold?" "I'll tell you!" cried Tom. "What noise was that?" said the thief, frightened; "I'm sure I heard someone speak." They stood still listening, and Tom said, "Take me with you, and I'll soon show you how to get the parson's money." "But where are you?" said they. "Look about on the ground," answered he, "and listen where the sound comes from." At last the thieves found him out, and lifted him up in their hands. "You little urchin!" they said, "what can you do for us?" "Why, I can get between the iron window-bars of the parson's house, and throw you out whatever you want." "That's a good thought," said the thieves; "come along, we shall see what you can do."

When they came to the parson's house, Tom slipped through the window-bars into the room, and then called out as loud as he could bawl, "Will you have all that is here?" At this the thieves were frightened, and said, "Softly, softly! Speak low, that you may not awaken anybody." But Tom seemed as if he did not understand them, and bawled out again, "How much will you have? Shall I throw it all out?" Now the cook lay in the next room; and hearing a noise she raised herself up in her bed and listened. Meantime the thieves were frightened, and ran off a little way; but at last they plucked up their hearts, and said, "The little urchin is only trying to make fools of us." So they came back and whispered softly to him, saying, "Now let us have no more of your roguish jokes; but throw us out some of the money." Then Tom called out as loud as he could, "Very well! hold your hands! here it comes."

The cook heard this quite plain, so she sprang out of bed, and ran to open the door. The thieves ran off as if a wolf was at their tails: and the maid, having groped about and found nothing, went away for a light. By the time she came back, Tom had slipped off into the barn; and when she had looked about and searched every hole and corner, and found nobody, she went to bed, thinking she must have been dreaming with her eyes open.

The little man crawled about in the hayloft, and at last found a snug place to finish his night's rest in; so he laid himself down, meaning to sleep till daylight, and then find his way home to his father and mother. But alas! how woefully he was undone! what crosses and sorrows happen to us all in this world! The cook got up early, before daybreak, to feed the cows; and going straight to the hayloft, carried away a large bundle of hay, with the little man in the middle of it, fast asleep. He still, however, slept on, and did not awake till he found himself in the mouth of the cow; for the cook had put the hay into the cow's rick, and the cow had taken Tom up in a mouthful of it. "Good lack-a-day!" said he, "how came I to tumble into the mill?" But he soon found out where he really was; and was forced to have all his wits about him, that he might not get between the cow's teeth, and so be crushed to death. At last down he went into her stomach. "It is rather dark," said he; "they forgot to build windows in this room to let the sun in; a candle would be no bad thing."

Though he made the best of his bad luck, he did not like his quarters at all; and the worst of it was, that more and more hay was always coming down, and the space left for him became smaller and smaller. At last he cried out as loud as he could, "Don't bring me any more hay! Don't bring me any more hay!"

The maid happened to be just then milking the cow; and hearing someone speak, but seeing nobody, and yet being quite sure it was the same voice that she had heard in the night, she was so frightened that she fell off her stool, and overset the milk pail. As soon as she could pick herself up out of the dirt, she ran off as fast as she could to her master the parson, and said, "Sir, sir, the cow is talking!" But the parson said, "Woman, thou art surely mad!" However, he went with her into the cow-house, to try and see what was the matter.

Scarcely had they set foot on the threshold, when Tom called out, "Don't bring me any more hay!" Then the parson himself was frightened; and thinking the cow was surely bewitched, told his man to kill her on the spot. So the cow was killed, and cut up; and the stomach, in which Tom lay, was thrown out upon a dunghill.

Tom soon set himself to work to get out, which was not a very easy task; but at last, just as he had made room to get his head out, fresh ill-luck befell him. A hungry wolf sprang out, and swallowed up the whole stomach, with Tom in it, at one gulp, and ran away.

Tom, however, was still not disheartened; and thinking the wolf would not dislike having some chat with him as he was going along, he called out, "My good friend, I can show you a famous treat."

"Where's that?" said the wolf. "In such and such a house," said Tom, describing his own father's house. "You can crawl through the drain into the kitchen and then into the pantry, and there you will find cakes, ham, beef, cold chicken, roast pig, apple-dumplings, and everything that your heart can wish."

The wolf did not want to be asked twice; so that very night he went to the house and crawled through the drain into the kitchen, and then into the pantry, and ate and drank there to his heart's content. As soon as he had had enough he wanted to get away; but he had eaten so much that he could not go out by the same way he came in.

This was just what Tom had reckoned upon; and now he began to set up a great shout, making all the noise he could. "Will you be easy?" said the wolf; "you'll awaken everybody in the house if you make such a clatter." "What's that to me?" said the little man; "you have had your frolic, now I've a mind to be merry myself"; and he began singing and shouting as loud as he could.

The woodman and his wife, being awakened by the noise, peeped through a crack in the door; but when they saw a wolf was there, you may well suppose that they were sadly frightened; and the woodman ran for his axe, and gave his wife a scythe. "Do you stay behind," said the woodman, "and when I have knocked him on the head you must rip him up with the scythe." Tom heard all this, and cried out, "Father, father! I am here, the wolf has swallowed me." And his father said, "Heaven be praised! we have found our dear child again"; and he told his wife not to use the scythe for fear she should hurt him. Then he aimed a great blow, and struck the wolf on the head, and killed him on the spot! and when he was dead they cut open his body, and set Tommy free. "Ah!" said the father, "what fears we have had for you!" "Yes, father," answered he; "I have traveled all over the world, I think, in one way or other, since we parted; and now I am very glad to come home and get fresh air again." "Why, where have you been?" said his father. "I have been in a mouse-hole—and in a snail-shell—and down a cow's throat—and in the wolf's belly; and yet here I am again, safe and sound."

"Well," said they, "you are come back, and we will not sell you again for all the riches in the world."

Then they hugged and kissed their dear little son, and gave him plenty to eat and drink, for he was very hungry; and then they fetched new clothes for him, for his old ones had been quite spoiled on his journey. So Master Thumb stayed at home with his father and mother, in peace; for though he had been so great a traveler, and had done and seen so many fine things, and was fond enough of telling the whole story, he always agreed that, after all, there's no place like HOME!

POEMS

To an Insect

BY OLIVER WENDELL HOLMES

I love to hear thine earnest voice,
　Wherever thou art hid,
　Thou testy little dogmatist,
　Thou pretty Katydid!
Thou mindest me of gentlefolks,
　　　—
　Old gentlefolks are they, —
Thou say'st an undisputed thing
　In such a solemn way.

Thou art a female, Katydid!
　I know it by the trill
　That quivers through thy
　　piercing notes,
　So petulant and shrill,
I think there is a knot of you
Beneath the hollow tree, —
A knot of spinster Katydids, —
　Do Katydids drink tea?

Oh, tell me where did Katy live,
　And what did Katy do?
And was she very fair and young,
　And yet so wicked, too?
Did Katy love a naughty man,
Or kiss more cheeks than one?
I warrant Katy did no more
Than many a Kate has done.

Dear me! I'll tell you all about
　My fuss with little Jane,
And Ann, with whom I used to
　　walk
　So often down the lane,
And all that tore their locks of
　　black,
Or wet their eyes of blue, —
Pray tell me, sweetest Katydid,
　What did poor Katy do?

Ah no! the living oak shall crash,
　That stood for ages still,
The rock shall rend its mossy base
　And thunder down the hill,
　Before the little Katydid
　Shall add one word, to tell
The mystic story of the maid
Whose name she knows so well.

Peace to the ever murmuring
　　race!
　And when the latest one
Shall fold in death her feeble
　　wings
　Beneath the autumn sun,
Then shall she raise her fainting
　　voice,
　And lift her drooping lid,
And then the child of future years
　Shall hear what Katy did.

Rumpelstiltskin

BY THE BROTHERS GRIMM

y the side of a wood, in a country a long way off, ran a fine stream of water; and upon the stream there stood a mill. The miller's house was close by, and the miller, you must know, had a very beautiful daughter. She was, moreover, very shrewd and clever; and the miller was so proud of her, that he one day told the king of the land, who used to come and hunt in the wood, that his daughter could spin gold out of straw. Now this king was very fond of money; and when he heard the miller's boast his greediness was raised, and he sent for the girl to be brought before him. Then he led her to a chamber in his palace where there was a great heap of straw, and gave her a spinning-wheel, and said, "All this must be spun into gold before morning, as you love your life." It was in vain that the poor maiden said that it was only a silly boast of her father, for that she could do no such thing as spin straw into gold: the chamber door was locked, and she was left alone.

She sat down in one corner of the room, and began to bewail her hard fate; when on a sudden the door opened, and a droll-looking little man hobbled in, and said, "Good morrow to you, my good lass; what are you weeping for?" "Alas!" said she, "I must spin this straw into gold, and I know not how." "What will you give me," said the hobgoblin, "to do it for you?" "My necklace," replied the maiden. He took her at her word, and sat himself down to the wheel, and whistled and sang:

"Round about, round about,
Lo and behold!
Reel away, reel away,
Straw into gold!"

And round about the wheel went merrily; the work was quickly done, and the straw was all spun into gold.

When the king came and saw this, he was greatly astonished and pleased; but his heart grew still more greedy of gain, and he shut up the poor miller's daughter again with a fresh task. Then she knew not what to do, and sat down once more to weep; but the dwarf soon opened the door, and said, "What will you give me to do your task?" "The ring on my finger," said she. So her little friend took the ring, and began to work at the wheel again, and whistled and sang:

"Round about, round about,

Lo and behold!

Reel away, reel away,

Straw into gold!"

Till, long before morning, all was done again.

The king was greatly delighted to see all this glittering treasure; but still he had not enough: so he took the miller's daughter to a yet larger heap, and said, "All this must be spun tonight; and if it is, you shall be my queen." As soon as she was alone that dwarf came in, and said, "What will you give me to spin gold for you this third time?" "I have nothing left," said she. "Then say you will give me," said the little man, "the first little child that you may have when you are queen." "That may never be," thought the miller's daughter: and as she knew no other way to get her task done, she said she would do what he asked. Round went the wheel again to the old song, and the manikin once more spun the heap into gold. The king came in the morning, and, finding all he wanted, was forced to keep his word; so he married the miller's daughter, and she really became queen.

At the birth of her first little child she was very glad, and forgot the dwarf, and what she had said. But one day he came into her room, where she was sitting playing with her baby, and put her in mind of it. Then she grieved sorely at her misfortune, and said she would give him all the wealth of the kingdom if he would let her off, but in vain; till at last her tears softened him, and he said, "I will give you three days' grace, and if during that time you tell me my name, you shall keep your child."

Now the queen lay awake all night, thinking of all the odd names that she had ever heard; and she sent messengers all over the land to find out new ones. The next day the little man came, and she began with Timothy, Ichabod, Benjamin, Jeremiah, and all the names she could remember; but to all and each of them he said, "Madam, that is not my name."

The second day she began with all the comical names she could hear of, Bandy-Legs, Hunchback, Crook-Shanks, and so on; but the little gentleman still said to every one of them, "Madam, that is not my name."

The third day one of the messengers came back, and said, "I have traveled two days without hearing of any other names; but yesterday, as I was climbing a high hill, among the trees of the forest where the fox and the hare bid each other good night, I saw a little hut; and before the hut burnt a fire; and round about the fire a funny little dwarf was dancing upon one leg, and singing:

'Merrily the feast I'll make.

Today I'll brew, tomorrow bake;

Merrily I'll dance and sing,

For next day will a stranger bring.

Little does my lady dream

Rumpelstiltskin is my name!'"

When the queen heard this she jumped for joy, and as soon as her little friend came she sat down upon her throne, and called all her court round to enjoy the fun; and the nurse stood by her side with the baby in her arms, as if it was quite ready to be given up. Then the little man began to chuckle at the thought of having the poor child, to take home with him to his hut in the woods; and he cried out, "Now, lady, what is my name?" "Is it John?" asked she.

"No, madam!" "Is it Tom?" "No, madam!" "Is it Jemmy?" "It is not." "Can your name be *Rumpelstiltskin*?" said the lady slyly. "Some witch told you that! —some witch told you that!" cried the little man, and dashed his right foot in a rage so deep into the floor, that he was forced to lay hold of it with both hands to pull it out.

Then he made the best of his way off, while the nurse laughed and the baby crowed; and all the court jeered at him for having had so much trouble for nothing, and said, "We wish you a very good morning, and a merry feast, Mr Rumpelstiltskin!"

HOW TO SAY "I LOVE YOU" IN DIFFERENT LANGUAGES

- **Afrikaans:** Ek het jou lief
- **Albanian:** Te dua
- **Armenian:** Yes kez si'rumem
- **Cantonese:** Ngo oi ney
- **Creole:** Mi aime jou
- **Danish:** Jeg elsker dig
- **Dutch:** Ik hou van jou
- **English:** I love you
- **Filipino:** Iniibig kita
- **Finnish:** ina rakastan sinua
- **French:** Je t'aime
- **German:** Ich liebe dich
- **Greek:** S'agapo
- **Hawaiian:** Aloha wau ia 'oe
- **Hungarian:** Szeretlek te'ged
- **Icelandic:** Eg elska thig
- **Indonesian:** Saya cinta pad-amu
- **Irish/Gaelic:** Taim i' ngra leat
- **Italian:** Ti amo
- **Japanese:** Kimi o ai shiteru
- **Korean:** Dangsinul sarang-hee yo
- **Malaysian:** Saya cinta mu
- **Mandarin:** Wo ay ni
- **Norwegian:** Jeg elsker deg
- **Polish:** Kocham cie
- **Portuguese (Brazilian):** Eu te amo
- **Romanian:** Te iubesc
- **Russian:** Ya lyublyu tyebya
- **Spanish:** Te amoSwahili: Nakupenda
- **Swedish:** Jag älskar dig
- **Ukrainian:** Ya tebe kokhaju
- **Vietnamese:** Toi yeu em

CLASSIC MOTHER-SON MOVIES

- *Home Alone*
- *Where the Wild Things Are*
- *The Incredibles*
- *Dumbo*
- *E.T. The Extra-Terrestrial*
- *Happy Feet*
- *Bambi*
- *Willy Wonka & the Chocolate Factory*
- *Peter Pan*
- *The Blind Side*
- *Rookie of the Year*
- *Mars Needs Moms*

The Elves and the Shoemaker

BY THE BROTHERS GRIMM

here was once a shoemaker, who worked very hard and was very honest: but still he could not earn enough to live upon; and at last all he had in the world was gone, save just leather enough to make one pair of shoes.

Then he cut his leather out, all ready to make up the next day, meaning to rise early in the morning to his work. His conscience was clear and his heart light amidst all his troubles; so he went peaceably to bed, left all his cares to Heaven, and soon fell asleep. In the morning after he had said his prayers, he sat himself down to his work; when, to his great wonder, there stood the shoes all ready made, upon the table. The good man knew not what to say or think at such an odd thing happening. He looked at the workmanship; there was not one false stitch in the whole job; all was so neat and true, that it was quite a masterpiece.

The same day a customer came in, and the shoes suited him so well that he willingly paid a price higher than usual for them; and the poor shoemaker, with the money, bought leather enough to make two pairs more. In the evening he cut out the work, and went to bed early, that he might get up and begin betimes next day; but he was saved all the trouble, for when he got up in the morning the work was done ready to his hand. Soon in came buyers, who paid him handsomely for his goods, so that he bought leather enough for four pair more. He cut out the work again overnight and found it done in the morning, as before; and so it went on for some time: what was got ready in the evening was always done by daybreak, and the good man soon became thriving and well off again.

One evening, about Christmas-time, as he and his wife were sitting over the fire chatting together, he said to her, "I should like to sit up and watch tonight, that we may see who it is that comes and does my work for me." The wife liked the thought; so they left a light burning, and hid themselves in a corner of the room, behind a curtain that was hung up there, and watched what would happen.

As soon as it was midnight, there came in two little naked dwarfs; and they sat themselves upon the shoemaker's bench, took up all the work that was cut out, and began to ply with their little fingers, stitching and rapping and tapping away at such a rate, that the shoemaker was all wonder, and could not take his eyes off them. And on they went, till the job was quite done, and the shoes stood ready for use upon the table. This was long before daybreak; and then they bustled away as quick as lightning.

The next day the wife said to the shoemaker, "These little wights have made us rich, and we ought to be thankful to them, and do them a good turn if we can. I am quite sorry to see them run about as they do; and indeed it is not very decent, for they have nothing upon their backs to keep off the cold. I'll tell you what, I will make each of them a shirt, and a coat and waistcoat, and a pair of pantaloons into the bargain; and do you make each of them a little pair of shoes."

The thought pleased the good cobbler very much; and one evening, when all the things were ready, they laid them on the table, instead of the work that they used to cut out, and then went and hid themselves, to watch what the little elves would do.

About midnight in they came, dancing and skipping, hopped round the room, and then went to sit down to their work as usual; but when they saw the clothes lying for them, they laughed and chuckled, and seemed mightily delighted.

Then they dressed themselves in the twinkling of an eye, and danced and capered and sprang about, as merry as could be; till at last they danced out at the door, and away over the green.

The good couple saw them no more; but everything went well with them from that time forward, as long as they lived.

How to Play War

ard games are a good old-fashioned way to spend time together with your son and a great family tradition. Shuffle the deck and let the games begin!

What You'll Need:

A standard deck of fifty-two playing cards; two to four players.

Objective:

To win all the cards. The game continues until there is one player left with cards, and that player wins the game!

To Play:

Begin by shuffling the deck of cards. Deal the cards face down so each player has twenty-six cards. Do not look at your cards; just keep them in a pile in front of you.

The game begins with each player turning over their top card at the same time. Suits are ignored and an Ace ranks as high, a 2 as low. Whoever has the higher card wins both cards, and places them face down at the bottom of their pile.

Along the way, if two (or more) players turn over the same card (e.g., they both put down a 5), then there is a war between those players. The flipped cards stay on the table, and on top of those cards, three new cards are placed face down. When those three cards have been placed, each player turns over a fourth card face up. The highest card wins the piles of cards, and the game continues; if the cards turned over are the same again, the war continues. The first player to run out of cards drops out, and so on. The last player with cards remaining is the winner!

Note: If you do not have enough cards to fight the war, you must forfeit. If both players do not have enough cards, whoever runs out of cards first loses.

How to Play Go Fish

efore you begin: You'll need two to six players; a standard deck of 52 playing cards.

Objective: To win the most sets of pairs.

To Play:

Begin by shuffling the deck and dealing seven cards face down to each player. (If more than four people are playing, deal only five cards to each player.)

Place the remaining cards face down in the middle of the table. This is the "go fish" pond.

Players can pick up their cards. If they have any pairs, they can lay them down in front of them before the game begins.

The player to the left of the dealer goes first; play then passes to the player on his or her left, etc.

To begin, Player 1 asks another player of their choosing if they have a specific card (e.g., "Bobby, do you have a 3?"). If the player has the card being requested, he must give it to Player 1, who displays the pair face up on the table in front of them.

If the player does not have the card Player 1 has requested, they respond with "Go fish." Player 1 then takes the top card in the "fish pond" and adds it to his or her hand of cards. (If the card on the top of the pile is the card Player 1 was looking for, he or she says "Fish, fish, I got my wish!" and receives another turn.)

The player who matches all of their cards into pairs first is the winner!

Learning about gardening is a great way to cultivate a love for nature in your son . . . and a great excuse to get your hands dirty together!

What You'll Need:

First you'll need to decide what you'd like to plant together! These are some of the flowers and herbs that are easily grown indoors:

Flowers: Miniature roses, pansies, impatiens, dwarf sunflowers, nasturtiums, petunias, geraniums, marigolds

Herbs: Basil, parsley, chives, mint, lavender, oregano, rosemary, sage, thyme, tarragon

1. Next you'll need to find a container to plant your seeds in. A terra cotta pot works well, along with plastic or ceramic pots. But you can be as creative as you'd like. Old mugs, pots and pans, a sand pail, baskets (with a liner, of course), cookie jars, and coffee cans would all make for interesting planters! If you choose an unconventional container that you cannot make drainage holes in, add some rocks (or even marbles) in the bottom to provide drainage for the soil. Make sure there is something underneath your "pot" to catch any extra water.

2. Once you have your container, fill it with potting soil, leaving a few inches at the top. You can buy potting soil that is perfect for indoor planting at any garden center. Don't pack the soil in too tight, just give it a shake and let the soil settle in.

3. Now it's time to plant! Drop the seeds you've chosen on top of the soil, then cover with another ½" layer of earth.

4. Leave them to grow in a sunny window, remembering to water your flowers when the soil feels dry!

POLLY WOLLY DOODLE

Oh, I went down South
For to see my Sal
Sing Polly wolly doodle all the day
My Sal, she is a spunky gal
Sing Polly wolly doodle all the day

(Chorus:) Fare thee well, Fare thee well,
Fare thee well my fairy fay
For I'm going to Lou'siana For to see my Susyanna
Sing Polly wolly doodle all the day

Oh, my Sal, she is a maiden fair
Sing Polly wolly doodle all the day
With curly eyes and laughing hair
Sing Polly wolly doodle all the day

(Chorus)

Behind the barn, Down on my knees
Sing Polly wolly doodle all the day
I thought I heard A chicken sneeze
Sing Polly wolly doodle all the day

(Chorus)

He sneezed so hard with the whooping cough
Sing Polly wolly doodle all the day
He sneezed his head and his tail right off
Sing Polly wolly doodle all the day

(Chorus)

Oh, a grasshopper sittin' On a railroad track
Sing Polly wolly doodle all the day
A-pickin' his teeth
With a carpet tack
Sing Polly wolly doodle all the day

(Chorus)

Oh, I went to bed But it wasn't any use
Sing Polly wolly doodle all the day
My feet stuck out Like a chicken roost
Sing Polly wolly doodle all the day

(Chorus)

The Leaping Match

BY HANS CHRISTIAN ANDERSEN

 he Flea, the Grasshopper, and the Frog once wanted to see which of them could jump the highest. They made a festival, and invited the whole world and every one else besides who liked to come and see the grand sight. Three famous jumpers they were, as all should say, when they met together in the room.

"I will give my daughter to him who shall jump highest," said the King; "it would be too bad for you to have the jumping, and for us to offer no prize."

The Flea was the first to come forward. He had most exquisite manners, and bowed to the company on every side; for he was of noble blood, and, besides, was accustomed to the society of man, and that, of course, had been an advantage to him.

Next came the Grasshopper. He was not quite so elegantly formed as the Flea, but he knew perfectly well how to conduct himself, and he wore the green uniform which belonged to him by right of birth. He said, moreover, that he came of a very ancient Egyptian family, and that in the house where he then lived he was much thought of.

The fact was that he had been just brought out of the fields and put in a card-house three stories high, and built on purpose for him, with the colored sides inwards, and doors and windows cut out of the Queen of Hearts. "And I sing so well," said he, "that sixteen parlor-bred crickets, who have chirped from infancy and yet got no one to build them card-houses to live in, have fretted themselves thinner even than before, from sheer vexation on hearing me."

It was thus that the Flea and the Grasshopper made the most of themselves, each thinking himself quite an equal match for the princess.

The Leapfrog said not a word; but people said that perhaps he thought the more; and the housedog who snuffed at him with his nose allowed that he was of good family. The old councilor, who had had three orders given him in vain for keeping quiet, asserted that the Leapfrog was a prophet, for that one could see on his back whether the coming winter was to be severe or mild, which is more than one can see on the back of the man who writes the almanac.

"I say nothing for the present," exclaimed the King; "yet I have my own opinion, for I observe everything."

And now the match began. The Flea jumped so high that no one could see what had become of him; and so they insisted that he had not jumped at all—which was disgraceful after all the fuss he had made.

The Grasshopper jumped only half as high; but he leaped into the King's face, who was disgusted by his rudeness.

The Leapfrog stood for a long time, as if lost in thought; people began to think he would not jump at all.

"I'm afraid he is ill!" said the dog and he went to snuff at him again; when lo! he suddenly made a sideways jump into the lap of the princess, who sat close by on a little golden stool.

"There is nothing higher than my daughter," said the King; "therefore to bound into her lap is the highest jump that can be made. Only one of good understanding would ever have thought of that. Thus the Frog has shown that he has sense. He has brains in his head, that he has."

And so he won the princess.

"I jumped the highest, for all that," said the Flea; "but it's all the same to me. The princess may have the stiff-legged, slimy creature, if she likes. In this world merit seldom meets its reward. Dullness and heaviness win the day. I am too light and airy for a stupid world."

And so the Flea went into foreign service.

The Grasshopper sat without on a green bank and reflected on the world and its ways; and he too said, "Yes, dullness and heaviness win the day; a fine exterior is what people care for nowadays." And then he began to sing in his own peculiar way—and it is from his song that we have taken this little piece of history, which may very possibly be all untrue, although it does stand printed here in black and white.

BEDTIME PRAYERS

Now I Lay Me Down

Now I lay me down to sleep,
I pray the Lord my soul to keep,
Lord, be with me through
the night
And keep me 'til the
morning light.

Grace

Thank you for the world
so sweet,
Thank you for the food we eat.
Thank you for the birds that sing,
Thank you, God, for everything.
—E. Rutter Leatham

A Child's Evening Hymn

I hear no voice, I feel no touch,
I see no glory bright;
But yet I know that God is near,
In darkness as in light.
God watches ever by my side,
And hears my whispered prayer:
A God of love for a little child
Both night and day does care.

Angel Blessing at Bedtime

Angels bless and angels keep
Angels guard me while I sleep
Bless my heart and bless
my home
Bless my spirit as I roam
Guide and guard me through
the night
and wake me with the
morning's light.
Amen

TOYS OVER TIME

1900s

- The Lionel train set, tin toys, wind-up toys, Crayola crayons, baseball cards, jigsaw puzzles

1910s

- The Erector set, Lincoln logs, Tinker Toys

1920s

- Pogo sticks, the Duncan Yo-Yo, TootsieToy cars, die cast cars/boats/planes/trains

1930s

- The Viewmaster, Scrabble, Monopoly

1940s

- Model airplanes, Slinkies, Silly Putty, bubbles, rocking horse, Tonka trucks

1950s

- Walkie-talkies, Yahtzee, toy telephones, ant farms, Play-doh, Frisbee, Mr. Potato Head

1960s

- Etch A Sketch, Lego, G. I. Joe, Twister, Hot Wheels, Big Wheels

1970s

- Skateboards, Star Wars action figures, Atari video games, Rubik's Cube, Weebles

1980s

- Teenage Mutant Ninja Turtles, Nintendo video games, Super Soakers

GAMES TO PLAY WITH YOUR LITTLE BOY

- Hide-and-Go-Seek
- Tag
- Four Square
- Duck, Duck, Goose
- Red Light, Green Light
- Follow the Leader
- Leapfrog
- Jacks
- Pick-Up Sticks
- Red Rover
- Tug of War
- Capture the Flag
- Stop and Go
- Monkey in the Middle
- Marbles
- Kick the Can
- Simon Says
- Hot Potato
- Freeze Tag

Even when freshly washed and relieved of all obvious confections, children tend to be sticky.

——FRAN LEBOWITZ

I'VE BEEN WORKING ON THE RAILROAD

I've been working on the railroad
All the livelong day
I've been working on the railroad
Just to pass the time away

Can't you hear the whistle blowing
Rise up so early in the morn
Can't you hear the captain shouting

Dinah, blow your horn
Dinah, won't you blow
Dinah, won't you blow
Dinah, won't you blow your horn
Dinah, won't you blow
Dinah, won't you blow

Dinah, won't you blow your horn

Someone's in the kitchen with Dinah
Someone's in the kitchen I know
Someone's in the kitchen with Dinah
Strumming on the old banjo, and singing

Fie, fi, fiddly i o
Fie, fi, fiddly i o
Fie, fi, fiddly i o
Strumming on the old banjo

ROW, ROW, ROW YOUR BOAT

Row, row, row your boat
Gently down the stream.
Merrily, merrily, merrily, merrily,
Life is but a dream.

The Prince and the Dragon

FROM *VOLKSMAREHEN DER SERBEN*

 nce upon a time there lived an emperor who had three sons. They were all fine young men, and fond of hunting, and scarcely a day passed without one or other of them going out to look for game.

One morning the eldest of the three princes mounted his horse and set out for a neighbouring forest, where wild animals of all sorts were to be found. He had not long left the castle, when a hare sprang out of a thicket and dashed across the road in front. The young man gave chase at once, and pursued it over hill and dale, till at last the hare took refuge in a mill which was standing by the side of a river. The prince followed and entered the mill, but stopped in terror by the door, for, instead of a hare, before him stood a dragon, breathing fire and flame. At this fearful sight the prince turned to fly, but a fiery tongue coiled round his waist, and drew him into the dragon's mouth, and he was seen no more.

A week passed away, and when the prince never came back everyone in the town began to grow uneasy. At last his next brother told the emperor that he likewise would go out to hunt, and that perhaps he would find some clue as to his brother's disappearance. But hardly had the castle gates closed on the prince than the hare sprang out of the bushes as before, and led the huntsman up hill and down dale, till they reached the mill. Into this the hare flew with the prince at his heels, when, lo! instead of the hare, there stood a dragon breathing fire and flame; and out shot a fiery tongue which coiled round the prince's waist, and lifted him straight into the dragon's mouth, and he was seen no more.

Days went by, and the emperor waited and waited for the sons who never came, and could not sleep at night for wondering where they were and what had become of them. His youngest son wished to go in search of his brothers, but for long the emperor refused to listen to him, lest he should lose him also. But the prince prayed so hard for leave to make the search, and promised so often that he would be very cautious and careful, that at length the emperor gave him permission, and ordered the best horse in the stables to be saddled for him.

Full of hope the young prince started on his way, but no sooner was he outside the city walls than a hare sprang out of the bushes and ran before him, till they reached the mill. As before, the animal dashed in through the open door, but this time he was not followed by the prince. Wiser than his brothers, the young man turned away, saying to himself: "There are as good hares in the forest as any that have come out of it, and when I have caught them, I can come back and look for you."

For many hours he rode up and down the mountain, but saw nothing, and at last, tired of waiting, he went back to the mill. Here he found an old woman sitting, whom he greeted pleasantly.

"Good morning to you, little mother," he said; and the old woman answered: "Good morning, my son."

"Tell me, little mother," went on the prince, "where shall I find my hare?"

"My son," replied the old woman, "that was no hare, but a dragon who has led many men hither, and then has eaten them all." At these words the prince's heart grew heavy, and he cried, "Then my brothers must have come here, and have been eaten by the dragon!"

"You have guessed right," answered the old woman; "and I can give you no better counsel than to go home at once, before the same fate overtakes you."

"Will you not come with me out of this dreadful place?" said the young man.

"He took me prisoner, too," answered she, "and I cannot shake off his chains."

"Then listen to me," cried the prince. "When the dragon comes back, ask him where he always goes when he leaves here, and what makes him so strong; and when you have coaxed the secret from him, tell me the next time I come."

So the prince went home, and the old woman remained in the mill, and as soon as the dragon returned she said to him:

"Where have you been all this time—you must have traveled far?"

"Yes, little mother, I have indeed traveled far," answered he. Then the old woman began to flatter him, and to praise his cleverness; and when she thought she had got him into a good temper, she said: "I have wondered so often where you get your strength from; I do wish you would tell me. I would stoop and kiss the place out of pure love!" The dragon laughed at this, and answered:

"In the hearthstone yonder lies the secret of my strength."

Then the old woman jumped up and kissed the hearth; whereat the dragon laughed the more, and said:

"You foolish creature! I was only jesting. It is not in the hearthstone, but in that tall tree that lies the secret of my strength." Then the old woman jumped up again and put her arms round the tree, and kissed it heartily. Loudly laughed the dragon when he saw what she was doing.

"Old fool," he cried, as soon as he could speak, "did you really believe that my strength came from that tree?"

"Where is it then?" asked the old woman, rather crossly, for she did not like being made fun of.

"My strength," replied the dragon, "lies far away; so far that you could never reach it. Far, far from here is a kingdom, and by its capital city is a lake, and in the lake is a dragon, and inside the dragon is a wild boar, and inside the wild boar is a pigeon, and inside the pigeon a sparrow, and inside the sparrow is my strength." And when the old woman heard this, she thought it was no use flattering him any longer, for never, never, could she take his strength from him.

The following morning, when the dragon had left the mill, the prince came back, and the old woman told him all that the creature had said. He listened in silence, and then returned to the castle, where he put on a suit of shepherd's clothes, and taking a staff in his hand, he went forth to seek a place as tender of sheep.

For some time he wandered from village to village and from town to town, till he came at length to a large city in a distant kingdom, surrounded on three sides by a great lake, which happened to be the very lake in which the dragon lived. As was his custom, he stopped everybody whom he met in the streets that looked likely to want a shepherd and begged them to engage him, but they all seemed to have shepherds of their own, or else not to need any. The prince was beginning to lose heart, when a man who had overheard his question turned round and said that he had better go and ask the emperor, as he was in search of some one to see after his flocks.

"Will you take care of my sheep?" said the emperor, when the young man knelt before him.

"Most willingly, your Majesty," answered the young man, and he listened obediently while the emperor told him what he was to do.

"Outside the city walls," went on the emperor, "you will find a large lake, and by its banks lie the richest meadows in my kingdom. When you are leading out your flocks to pasture, they will all run straight to these meadows, and none that have gone there have ever been known to come back. Take heed, therefore, my son, not to suffer your sheep to go where they will, but drive them to any spot that you think best."

With a low bow the prince thanked the emperor for his warning, and promised to do his best to keep the sheep safe. Then he left the palace and went to the marketplace, where he bought two greyhounds, a hawk, and a set of pipes; after that he took the sheep out to pasture. The instant the animals caught sight of the lake lying before them, they trotted off as fast as their legs would go to the green meadows lying round it. The prince did not try to stop them; he only placed his hawk on the branch of a tree, laid his pipes on the grass, and bade the greyhounds sit still; then, rolling up his sleeves and trousers, he waded into the water crying as he did so: "Dragon! dragon! if you are not a coward, come out and fight with me!" And a voice answered from the depths of the lake:

"I am waiting for you, O prince"; and the next minute the dragon reared himself out of the water, huge and horrible to see. The prince sprang upon him and they grappled with each other and fought together till the sun was high, and it was noonday. Then the dragon gasped:

"O prince, let me dip my burning head once into the lake, and I will hurl you up to the top of the sky." But the prince answered:

"Oh, ho! my good dragon, do not crow too soon! If the emperor's daughter were only here, and would kiss me on the forehead, I would throw you up higher still!" And suddenly the dragon's hold loosened, and he fell back into the lake.

As soon as it was evening, the prince washed away all signs of the fight, took his hawk upon his shoulder, and his pipes under his arm, and with his greyhounds in front and his flock following after him he set out for the city. As they all passed through the streets the people stared in wonder, for never before had any flock returned from the lake.

The next morning he rose early, and led his sheep down the road to the lake. This time, however, the emperor sent two men on horseback to ride behind him, with orders to watch the prince all day long.

The horsemen kept the prince and his sheep in sight, without being seen themselves. As soon as they beheld the sheep running towards the meadows, they turned aside up a steep hill, which overhung the lake. When the shepherd reached the place he laid, as before, his pipes on the grass and bade the greyhounds sit beside them, while the hawk he perched on the branch of the tree. Then he rolled up his trousers and his sleeves, and waded into the water crying:

"Dragon! dragon! if you are not a coward, come out and fight with me!" And the dragon answered:

"I am waiting for you, O prince," and the next minute he reared himself out of the water, huge and horrible to see. Again they clasped each other tight round the body and fought till it was noon, and when the sun was at its hottest, the dragon gasped:

"O prince, let me dip my burning head once in the lake, and I will hurl you up to the top of the sky." But the prince answered:

"Oh, ho! my good dragon, do not crow too soon! If the emperor's daughter were only here, and would kiss me on the forehead, I would throw you up higher still!" And suddenly the dragon's hold loosened, and he fell back into the lake.

As soon as it was evening the prince again collected his sheep, and playing on his pipes he marched before them into the city. When he passed through the gates all the people came out of their houses to stare in wonder, for never before had any flock returned from the lake.

Meanwhile the two horsemen had ridden quickly back, and told the emperor all that they had seen and heard. The emperor listened eagerly to their tale, then called his daughter to him and repeated it to her.

"Tomorrow," he said, when he had finished, "you shall go with the shepherd to the lake, and then you shall kiss him on the forehead as he wishes."

But when the princess heard these words, she burst into tears, and sobbed out:

"Will you really send me, your only child, to that dreadful place, from which most likely I shall never come back?"

"Fear nothing, my little daughter, all will be well. Many shepherds have gone to that lake and none have ever returned; but this one has in these two days fought twice with the dragon and has escaped without a wound. So I hope tomorrow he will kill the dragon altogether, and deliver this land from the monster who has slain so many of our bravest men."

Scarcely had the sun begun to peep over the hills next morning, when the princess stood by the shepherd's side, ready to go to the lake. The shepherd was brimming over with joy, but the princess only wept bitterly. "Dry your tears, I implore you," said he. "If you will just do what I ask you, and when the time comes, run and kiss my forehead, you have nothing to fear."

Merrily the shepherd blew on his pipes as he marched at the head of his flock, only stopping every now and then to say to the weeping girl at his side:

"Do not cry so, Heart of Gold; trust me and fear nothing." And so they reached the lake.

In an instant the sheep were scattered all over the meadows, and the prince placed his hawk on the tree, and his pipes on the grass, while he bade his greyhounds lie beside them. Then he rolled up his trousers and his sleeves, and waded into the water, calling:

"Dragon! dragon! if you are not a coward, come forth, and let us have one more fight together." And the dragon answered: "I am waiting for you, O prince"; and the next minute he reared himself out of the water, huge and horrible to see. Swiftly he drew near to the bank, and the prince sprang to meet him, and they grasped each other round the body and fought till it was noon. And when the sun was at its hottest, the dragon cried:

"O prince, let me dip my burning head in the lake, and I will hurl you to the top of the sky." But the prince answered:

"Oh, ho! my good dragon, do not crow too soon! If the emperor's daughter were only here, and she would kiss my forehead, I would throw you higher still."

Hardly had he spoken, when the princess, who had been listening, ran up and kissed him on the forehead. Then the prince swung the dragon straight up into the clouds, and when he touched the earth again, he broke into a thousand pieces. Out of the pieces there sprang a wild boar and galloped away, but the prince called his hounds to give chase, and they caught the boar and tore it to bits. Out of the pieces there sprang a hare, and in a moment the greyhounds were after it, and they caught it and killed it; and out of the hare there came a pigeon. Quickly the prince let loose his hawk, which soared straight into the air, then swooped upon the bird and brought it to his master. The prince cut open its body and found the sparrow inside, as the old woman had said.

"Now," cried the prince, holding the sparrow in his hand, "now you shall tell me where I can find my brothers."

"Do not hurt me," answered the sparrow, "and I will tell you with all my heart. Behind your father's castle stands a mill, and in the mill are three slender twigs. Cut off these twigs and strike their roots with them, and the iron door of a cellar will open. In the cellar you will find as many people, young and old, women and children, as would fill a kingdom, and among them are your brothers."

By this time twilight had fallen, so the prince washed himself in the lake, took the hawk on his shoulder and the pipes under his arm, and with his greyhounds before him and his flock behind him, marched gaily into the town, the princess following them all, still trembling with fright. And so they passed through the streets, thronged with a wondering crowd, till they reached the castle.

Unknown to anyone, the emperor had stolen out on horseback, and had hidden himself on the hill, where he could see all that happened. When all was over, and the power of the dragon was broken for ever, he rode quickly back to the castle, and was ready to receive the prince with open arms, and to promise him his daughter to wife. The wedding took place with great splendor, and for a whole week the town was hung with colored lamps, and tables were spread in the hall of the castle for all who chose to come and eat. And when the feast was over, the prince told the emperor and the people who he really was, and at this everyone rejoiced still more, and preparations were made for the prince and princess to return to their own kingdom, for the prince was impatient to set free his brothers.

The first thing he did when he reached his native country was to hasten to the mill, where he found the three twigs as the sparrow had told him. The moment that he struck the root the iron door flew open, and from the cellar a countless multitude of men and women streamed forth. He bade them go one by one wheresoever they would, while he himself waited by the door till his brothers passed through. How delighted they were to meet again, and to hear all that the prince had done to deliver them from their enchantment. And they went home with him and served him all the days of their lives, for they said that he only who had proved himself brave and faithful was fit to be king.

CRAFT TIME
How to Make Your Own Fossils

You and your little archaeologist will love searching for different items to make fossil prints with. Let your creativity run wild as you dig in and make your very own unique fossils!

What You'll Need:
- ½ cup flour
- ½ cup used coffee grounds
- ¼ cup salt
- ¼ cup sand
- Water
- Fossil objects such as: sea shells, leaf, feather, toy dinosaurs, rocks, pine needles, ferns/foliage, cleaned bones (left over from chicken or meat)

1. Mix together all of the dry ingredients.

2. Add the water a little at a time until you have a thick dough-like consistency.

3. Flatten the dough to about an inch thick, and break the dough into the desired sizes.

4. Choose the objects you want to make into fossils and carefully press them into the dough.

5. Let your fossil dry completely and then share or display your findings!

Traditional Games for Boys

he games below have been favorites of little boys for centuries. Share your fond memories with your son and teach him how to play these classics!

KICK THE CAN
Before you begin:

You'll need at least four players; an empty tin can, soda can, or even an empty paint can or bucket (you can also use a ball, an empty plastic milk jug, or any other "kickable" object); and a large, safe, open space, like a field or yard, in which to play. (If supervised, it can also be played in a parking lot or at the end of a cul-de-sac.)

To play:

Draw straws or decide who the "counter" (also referred to as the "jailor," "ruler," "seeker," or "it") will be. All other players will be "hiders."

The game begins by the "can" being set upright in the middle of the play area, and the counter closing his or her eyes and counting to a decided-upon number. All of the other players hide.

The counter then sets out to find all the other players. If a player is found, the counter yells out that player's name and they race back to the can. If the hider kicks the can before the counter, the game starts again. But if the counter kicks the can first, then the hider is "caught," and he or she is sent "to the can" or "to jail," which is a designated area for the "captured" players, typically right near the can.

While the counter continues to look for players, the players can risk capture at any time and come out of hiding to try and kick the can. If a player can succeed without being tagged by the counter, the captives are set free from the can! The players then go hide again. But if the player is tagged before he or she can kick the can, he or she will be sent to the jail as well.

The game continues on until the counter has captured all the players, or until a found hider beats the counter back to the can!

FOUR SQUARE
Before you begin:
You'll need at least four people; chalk or tape; a rubber playground ball; and a flat concrete surface like a patio or driveway on which to play.

Make or draw a large ten-foot-square "court" and divide it into four equal quadrants. Number these smaller squares 1, 2, 3, and 4. Square 1 is the highest-ranking square; square 4 is the lowest. Make a diagonal line across the outside corner of square 1 to create a small triangle; this is where the ball will be served from.

The goal:
To move up by eliminating other players; to stay in, or move into, the number 1 square.

To play:
The player in square 1 begins by serving the ball into any other square. The ball must bounce once and the player in that square must hit the ball with their hand(s) into another square. The game continues until a player

- misses a ball
- hits a ball out of bounds
- allows the ball to bounce more than once in their square
- hits the ball into their own square
- catches or holds the ball instead of hitting it

A player who makes any of the above errors is eliminated, and players move up accordingly into the next highest-ranking square.

If there are more than four players, the new players step into the lowest square as players are eliminated.

The winner is the last person left, or whoever holds the server's position the longest in square 1!

POEMS

One, Two, Buckle My Shoe

One, two, buckle my shoe;
Three, four, knock at the door;
Five, six, pick up sticks;
Seven, eight, lay them straight;
Nine, ten, a good fat hen;
Eleven, twelve, dig and delve;
Thirteen, fourteen,
maids a-courting;
Fifteen, sixteen, maids in
the kitchen;
Seventeen, eighteen, maids
a-waiting;
Nineteen, twenty, my
plate's empty.

Wee Willie Winkie

Wee Willie Winkie runs
through the town,
Upstairs and downstairs, in his
nightgown,
Rapping at the window, crying
through the lock,
"Are the children in their beds?
Now it's eight o'clock."

Willie Winkie

BY WILLIAM MILLER

Hey! Willie Winkie,
Are you coming then?
The cat's singing gay tunes
To the sleeping hen.
The dog is lying on the floor,
And does not even peep;
But here's a wakeful laddie,
That will not fall asleep.
Anything but sleep, you rogue,
Glowing like the moon;
Rattling in a stone jug,
With an iron spoon.
Rumbling, tumbling all about
Crowing like a cock;
Screaming like I don't know what
Waking sleeping folks.
Hey! Willie Winkie!
Can't you keep him still,
Wriggling off a body's knee
Like a very eel.
That has with sleep a battle
Before he's done with play,
A wee, wee, dumpy, toddling lad
That runs the livelong day.

The Town Mouse and the Country Mouse, from Aesop's Fables

ow you must know that a Town Mouse once upon a time went on a visit to his cousin in the country. He was rough and ready, this cousin, but he loved his town friend and made him heartily welcome. Beans and bacon, cheese and bread, were all he had to offer, but he offered them freely. The Town Mouse rather turned up his long nose at this country fare, and said: "I cannot understand, Cousin, how you can put up with such poor food as this, but of course you cannot expect anything better in the country; come you with me and I will show you how to live. When you have been in town a week you will wonder how you could ever have stood a country life." No sooner said than done: the two mice set off for the town and arrived at the Town Mouse's residence late at night. "You will want some refreshment after our long journey," said the polite Town Mouse, and took his friend into the grand dining room. There they found the remains of a fine feast, and soon the two mice were eating up jellies and cakes and all that was nice. Suddenly they heard growling and barking. "What is that?" said the Country Mouse. "It is only the dogs of the house," answered the other. "Only!" said the Country Mouse. "I do not like that music at my dinner." Just at that moment the door flew open, in came two huge mastiffs, and the two mice had to scamper down and run off. "Good-bye, Cousin," said the Country Mouse, "What! going so soon?" said the other. "Yes," he replied;

"Better beans and bacon in peace than cakes and ale in fear."

Prepare for takeoff as you and your son investigate the art of making paper airplanes. Try this basic design and get ready to defy gravity!

What You'll Need:

- One 8.5" × 11" sheet of paper (almost any weight of paper will work, from computer paper to construction paper)
- A flat work surface and your hands!

1. Fold an 8.5" × 11" sheet of paper exactly in half the long way, and re-open it, creating two halves. The center line crease will be your guideline.

2. Position your unfolded paper flat in front of you so that the crease runs vertically. Take the top end of the paper and fold each of the two corners in towards the center so that the inside edges line up with the center line crease.

3. Fold the paper down on each side again so that the inside edges line up with the center crease.

4. Turn the paper airplane over and fold it in half again along the center line. You will now be looking at your plane from the side.

5. To make the wings, fold the upper edges down from the top of the plane, lining up the top fold with the center line (your original center fold is now the bottom of the plane). Turn over the plane and repeat on the other side to make the second wing.

6. You can also experiment with adding different folds in the wings of your plane or with the angles you throw your airplane! Get ready to fly!

A small son can charm himself into, and out of, most things.

——JENNY DE VRIES

Phone It In: How to Make a Tin Can Telephone

 his nostalgic craft is simple to make and fun to play with. Get ready for hours of entertainment and ingenuity with your tin can telephone! Now you're talking!

Before you begin:

You'll need: two tin cans, washed with the paper removed (be careful of sharp edges); a piece of string; a hammer and a nail (and an adult!)

To make the tin can telephone:

Turn the cans so the solid bottom is at the top. With the hammer and nail, make a hole in the bottom of each can just big enough for the string to get through.

Insert the string into each hole. Knot each end of the string inside each can.

Pull the string taut so that the knot is right up against the bottom of each can.

Now you can speak into one can while someone listens on the other end. The sound of your voice will vibrate across the string and into their ear!

LULLABIES

Hush, Little Baby

Hush, little baby,
don't say a word.
Papa's gonna buy you
a mockingbird
And if that mockingbird
won't sing,
Papa's gonna buy you a
diamond ring
And if that diamond
ring turns brass,
Papa's gonna buy you
a looking glass
And if that looking glass
gets broke,
Papa's gonna buy you a billy goat
And if that billy goat won't pull,
Papa's gonna buy you a
cart and bull
And if that cart and
bull turn over,
Papa's gonna buy you a dog
named Rover
And if that dog named
Rover won't bark
Papa's gonna buy you
a horse and cart
And if that horse and
cart fall down,

You'll still be the sweetest little
baby in town.

All the Pretty Horses

Hush-a-bye, don't you cry,
Go to sleep my little baby.
When you wake you shall have
All the pretty little horses.
Black and bays, dapples, grays,
All the pretty little horses.
Hush-a-bye, don't you cry,
Go to sleep my little baby.
Hush-a-bye, don't you cry,
Go to sleep my little baby.
When you wake you shall have
All the pretty little horses.

Brahms's Lullaby (Lullaby and Goodnight)

Lullaby and goodnight, with roses
bedight
With lilies o'er spread is
baby's wee bed
Lay thee down now and rest, may
thy slumber be blessed
Lay thee down now and rest, may
thy slumber be blessed

LULLABIES

Lullaby and goodnight, thy
mother's delight

Bright angels beside
my darling abide

They will guard thee at rest, thou
shalt wake on my breast

They will guard thee at rest, thou
shalt wake on my breast

Gaelic Lullaby
(traditional)

Hush the waves are rolling in,

White with foam, white
with foam;

Father toils amid the din;

But baby sleeps at home.

Hush the winds roar hoarse
and deep, —

On they come, on they come!

Brother seeks the
wandering sheep;

But baby sleeps at home.

Hush! the rain sweeps o'er the
knowes,

Where they roam,
where they roam;

Sister goes to seek the cows;

But baby sleeps at home.

Hush-a-Bye Baby

Hush-a-bye, Baby,
upon the tree top,

When the wind blows
the cradle will rock;

When the bough breaks the cradle
will fall,

Down tumbles cradle and
Baby, and all.

SING A SONG

THE FARMER IN THE DELL

The farmer in the dell,
The farmer in the dell,
Hi-ho, the derry-o,
The farmer in the dell.
The farmer takes a wife,
The farmer takes a wife,
Hi-ho, the derry-o,
The farmer takes a wife.
The wife takes a child,
The wife takes a child,
Hi-ho, the derry-o,
The wife takes a child.
The child takes a nurse,
The child takes a nurse,
Hi-ho, the derry-o,
The child takes a nurse.
The nurse takes the cow,
The nurse takes the cow,
Hi-ho, the derry-o,
The nurse takes the cow.
The cow takes a dog,

The cow takes a dog,
Hi-ho, the derry-o,
The cow takes a dog.
The dog takes a cat,
The dog takes a cat,
Hi-ho, the derry-o,
The dog takes a cat.
The cat takes a rat,
The cat takes a rat,
Hi-ho, the derry-o,
The cat takes a rat.
The rat takes the cheese,
The rat takes the cheese,
Hi-ho, the derry-o,
The rat takes the cheese
The cheese stands alone,
The cheese stands alone,
Hi-ho, the derry-o,
The cheese stands alone.

How to Make a Bug Habitat

 here's nothing more quintessential for boys than exploring the world of bugs and insects, and creating a bug habitat will make hunting for critters with your son even *more* fun!

Before you begin:

First you'll need to find something to put your bugs in. If you don't have a container specifically for bug hunting, any clear plastic container with a lid will work well. Just be sure to poke holes in the container or lid. You can also use a clear plastic produce container from the market, provided the bugs you catch are not smaller than the holes.

Next you'll need to create an environment that will be comfortable for your bugs to live in. Collect moss, grass, sticks, leaves, dirt, and rocks for your habitat. You'll want to put water in the habitat, too; a small container, like a bottle cap, filled with water will be sufficient.

To catch bugs:

Now it's time to go on a bug hunt! Look near grass, trees or bushes, under rocks, or near gardens, lakes, and ponds. Bugs are everywhere. You can use a small net or your hands to catch the bugs; gently place them in the habitat you've made.

Have fun observing your bugs and identifying what kinds of bugs you've found. Don't forget to release your bugs back into the wild when you're finished observing them!

POEMS

Come Out to Play

Girls and boys, come out to play,
The moon doth shine as
bright as day;
Leave your supper, and leave your
sleep,
And come with your playfellows
into the street.
Come with a whoop,
come with a call,
Come with a good will
or not at all.
Up the ladder and down the wall,
A half-penny roll will serve us all.
You find milk, and I'll find flour,
And we'll have a pudding in half
an hour.

Hide and Seek

BY WALTER DE LA MARE

Hide and seek, says the Wind,
In the shade of the woods;
Hide and seek, says the Moon,
To the hazel buds;
Hide and seek, says the Cloud,
Star on to star;
Hide and seek, says the Wave,
At the harbour bar;
Hide and seek, say I,
To myself, and step
Out of the dream of Wake
Into the dream of Sleep.

Three Blind Mice

Three blind mice!
See how they run!
They all ran after the farmer's
wife,
Who cut off their tails with a carv-
ing knife.
Did you ever see such a thing in
your life
As three blind mice?

Bedtime

The Man in the Moon looked out
of the moon,
Looked out of the moon and said,
"'Tis time for all children, on the
earth
To think about getting to bed."

The Little Shepherd Boy

nce upon a time there was a little shepherd boy who was famed far and wide for the wise answers which he gave to all questions. Now the King of the country heard of this lad, but he would not believe what was said about him, so the boy was ordered to come to court. When he arrived the King said to him: "If you can give me answers to each of the three questions which I will now put to you, I will bring you up as my own child, and you shall live here with me in my palace."

"What are these three questions?" asked the boy.

"The first is: How many drops of water are there in the sea?"

"My lord King," replied the shepherd boy, "let all the waters be stopped up on the earth, so that not one drop shall run into the sea before I count it, and then I will tell you how many drops there are in the sea!"

"The second question," said the King, "is: How many stars are there in the sky?"

"Give me a large sheet of paper," said the boy; and then he made in it with a pin so many minute holes that they were far too numerous to see or to count, and dazzled the eyes of whomsoever looked at them. This done, he said: "So many stars are there in the sky as there are holes in this paper; now count them." But nobody was able. Thereupon the King said: "The third question is: How many seconds are there in eternity?"

"In Lower Pomerania is situated the adamantine mountain, one mile in height, one mile in breadth, and one mile deep; and thither comes a bird once in every thousand years which rubs its beak against the hill, and, when the whole shall be rubbed away, then will the first second of eternity be gone by."

"You have answered the three questions like a sage," said the King, "and from henceforward you shall live with me in my palace, and I will treat you as my own child."

POEMS

A House of Cards
BY CHRISTINA ROSSETTI

A house of cards
Is neat and small:
Shake the table,
It must fall.

Find the Court cards
One by one;
Raise it, roof it,--
Now it's done:--
Shake the table!
That's the fun.

A Boy's Song
BY JAMES HOGG

Where the pools are
bright and deep,
Where the grey trout lies asleep,
Up the river and over the lea,
That's the way for Billy and me.

Where the blackbird sings
the latest,
Where the hawthorn blooms
the sweetest,
Where the nestlings
chirp and flee,
That's the way for Billy and me.

Where the mowers mow
the cleanest,
Where the hay lies thick
and greenest,
There to track the homeward
bee,
That's the way for Billy and me.

Where the hazel bank is steepest,
Where the shadow falls the
deepest,
Where the clustering nuts
fall free,
That's the way for Billy and me.

Why the boys should drive away
Little sweet maidens from the
play,
Or love to banter and fight
so well,
That's the thing I never could tell.

But this I know, I love to play
Through the meadow,
among the hay;
Up the water and over the lea,
That's the way for Billy and me.

CRAFT TIME
Make Your Own Play Dough

What You'll Need:

- 2 cups flour
- 2 cups warm water
- 1 cup salt
- 2 tablespoons vegetable oil
- 1 tablespoon cream of tartar
- Food coloring gel (if desired)

1. Mix all of the ingredients (except for the food coloring) together in a pot on the stove over low heat.

2. As you stir, the dough will thicken and then pull away from the sides to the center.

3. Continue to stir and cook until the dough is no longer sticky, but has a dry, dough-like texture.

4. Remove the dough so it can cool, and then knead the dough until there are no more lumps.

5. Now you are ready to color the play dough, if you'd like. Separate the dough into pieces and roll the pieces into balls. Then poke a hole into the center and use this hole to put a few drops of dye in. (This way the food coloring won't come into direct contact with your skin until you've worked it into the dough. You could use plastic wrap or gloves to work the food coloring through as well.) Knead the dough to distribute the dye, adding more food coloring until the desired color is reached.

Don't forget to store your play dough in an airtight container when you're done having fun!

POEMS

The Land of Counterpane
BY ROBERT LOUIS STEVENSON

When I was sick and lay a-bed,
I had two pillows at my head,
And all my toys beside me lay,
To keep me happy all the day.

And sometimes for an hour or so
I watched my leaden soldiers go,
With different uniforms
and drills,
Among the bedclothes,
through the hills;

And sometimes sent my
ships in fleets
All up and down among
the sheets;
Or brought my trees and
houses out,
And planted cities all about.

I was the giant great and still
That sits upon the pillow-hill,
And sees before him, dale
and plain,
The pleasant land of counterpane.

Where Go the Boats?
BY ROBERT LOUIS STEVENSON

Dark brown is the river,
Golden is the sand.
It flows along for ever,
With trees on either hand.

Green leaves a-floating,
Castles of the foam,
Boats of mine a-boating—
Where will all come home?

On goes the river
And out past the mill,
Away down the valley,
Away down the hill.

Away down the river,
A hundred miles or more,
Other little children
Shall bring my boats ashore.

Hold Down the Fort:
How to Make a Fort out of
Blankets and Pillows

 fort is the perfect place for your son to pretend and imagine, and building it together is half the fun!

Before you begin:

You'll need various blankets, pillows, sheets, couch cushions, chairs, and tables; stacks of books, clothespins, or rubber bands to secure the blankets.

To make your fort:

Decide what pieces of furniture you want to use; these will become the frame for your fort. Try to create height by using the back of a couch or a few dining room chairs as a wall; you could also use a broom as a tent pole to create height in your fort. You could also secure a rope across part of a room and hang a sheet over it to make a blanket tent; you could drape a blanket over a small table; or you could use your couch cushions to make a fort right on the couch!

Use your largest blanket or sheet to drape over the frame of your fort first. Secure the blankets with heavy objects or clothespins so that your fort is stable.

Arrange your blankets and pillows to cover up any holes.

Fill your fort with sleeping bags, a flashlight, and any other supplies you may need. Use your imagination! Your fort can become whatever you want it to be: a spaceship, a castle with a drawbridge, a tree house in the jungle, a pirate ship . . . anything!

POEMS

A Song About Myself (or The Naughty Boy)

BY JOHN KEATS

I.

There was a naughty boy,
A naughty boy was he,
He would not stop at home,
He could not quiet be —
He took
In his knapsack
A book
Full of vowels
And a shirt
With some towels,
A slight cap
For night cap,
A hair brush,
Comb ditto,
New stockings
For old ones
Would split O!
This knapsack
Tight at's back
He rivetted close
And followed his nose
To the north,
To the north,
And follow'd his nose
To the north.

II.

There was a naughty boy
And a naughty boy was he,
For nothing would he do
But scribble poetry —
He took
An ink stand
In his hand
And a pen
Big as ten
In the other,
And away
In a pother
He ran
To the mountains
And fountains
And ghostes
And postes
And witches
And ditches
And wrote
In his coat
When the weather
Was cool,
Fear of gout,
And without

POEMS

When the weather
Was warm —
Och the charm
When we choose
To follow one's nose
To the north,
To the north,
To follow one's nose
To the north!

Humpty Dumpty

Humpty Dumpty sat on a wall,
Humpty Dumpty had a great fall;
All the King's horses, and all the
King's men
Cannot put Humpty Dumpty
together again.

Jack and Jill

Jack and Jill went up the hill,
To fetch a pail of water;
Jack fell down, and broke
his crown,
And Jill came tumbling after.
Then up Jack got and
off did trot,
As fast as he could caper,

To old Dame Dob, who
patched his nob
With vinegar and brown paper.

Pat-a-Cake

Pat-a-cake, pat-a-cake,
Baker's man!
So I do, master,
As fast as I can.
Pat it, and prick it,
And mark it with T,
Put it in the oven
For Tommy and me.

Hickory Dickory Dock

Hickory, dickory, dock!
The mouse ran up the clock;
The clock struck one,
And down he run,
Hickory, dickory, dock!

BOOKS TO READ TO YOUR SON

Mystery, danger, love, excitement, fantasy! Here are some tales of faraway lands and places that can only be reached when you open a book and read with your son. Let your imaginations run wild together as you explore the worlds and unravel the stories beloved by boys for centuries.

- *Where the Wild Things Are* by Maurice Sendak
- *I'll Love You Forever* by Robert Munsch
- *Harold and the Purple Crayon* by Crockett Johnson
- *The Snowy Day* by Ezra Jack Keats
- *Charlie and the Chocolate Factory* by Roald Dahl
- *The Swiss Family Robinson* by Johann David Wyss
- *The Jungle Book* by Rudyard Kipling
- *The Giving Tree* by Shel Silverstein
- *Treasure Island* by Robert Louis Stevenson
- *Peter Pan* by J. M. Barrie
- *Stone Soup* by Marcia Brown
- *The Adventures of Huckleberry Finn* by Mark Twain
- *The Adventures of Tom Sawyer* by Mark Twain
- *James and the Giant Peach* by Roald Dahl

MOVIES YOUR LITTLE BOY WILL LOVE!

- *The Adventures of Huckleberry Finn*
- *The Sword in the Stone*
- *Oliver Twist*
- *The Jungle Book*
- *Old Yeller*
- *Stuart Little*
- *Lassie*
- *James and the Giant Peach*
- *The Rookie*
- *Hook*
- *Cars*
- *Monsters, Inc.*
- *E. T. The Extra-Terrestrial*
- *Peter Pan*
- *The Incredibles*
- *Up*
- *WALL-E*
- *Toy Story*
- *Charlie and the Chocolate Factory*
- *Tarzan*
- *Shrek*
- *Ratatouille*
- *The Rescuers Down Under*

Boy, n.:

a noise with dirt on it.

———Not Your Average Dictionary

POEMS

Simple Simon

Simple Simon met a pieman,
Going to the fair;
Says Simple Simon to the pieman,
"Let me taste your ware."
Says the pieman to Simple Simon,
"Show me first your penny."
Says Simple Simon to the pieman,
"Indeed, I have not any."
Simple Simon went a-fishing
For to catch a whale;
All the water he could find
Was in his mother's pail!
Simple Simon went to look
If plums grew on a thistle;
He pricked his fingers very much,
Which made poor Simon whistle.
He went to catch a dicky bird,
And thought he could not fail,
Because he had a little salt,
To put upon its tail.
He went for water in a sieve,
But soon it ran all through;
And now poor Simple Simon
Bids you all adieu.

The Muffin Man

Do you know the muffin man,
The muffin man, the muffin man,
Do you know the muffin man,
Who lives on Drury Lane?
Yes, I know the muffin man,
The muffin man, the muffin man,
Yes, I know the muffin man,
Who lives on Drury Lane.

Peter, Peter, Pumpkin Eater

Peter, Peter, pumpkin eater,
Had a wife and couldn't
keep her;
He put her in a pumpkin shell,
And then he kept her very well.
Peter, Peter pumpkin eater,
Had another, and didn't
love her;
Peter learned to read
and spell,
And then he loved
her very well.

POEMS

It's Raining, It's Pouring

It's raining; it's pouring.

The old man is snoring.

He went to bed and bumped
his head,

And he couldn't get up
in the morning.

The Crooked Sixpence

There was a crooked man, and he
went a crooked mile,

He found a crooked sixpence
beside a crooked stile;

He bought a crooked cat, which
caught a crooked mouse,

And they all lived together in a
little crooked house.

Baa, Baa, Black Sheep

Baa, baa, black sheep,

Have you any wool?

Yes, marry, have I,

Three bags full;

One for my master,

One for my dame,

But none for the little boy

Who cries in the lane.

Peter Piper

Peter Piper picked a peck of pickled peppers;

A peck of pickled peppers Peter
Piper picked;

If Peter Piper picked a peck of
pickled peppers,

Where's the peck of pickled peppers Peter Piper picked?

Little Boy Blue

Little Boy Blue, come,
blow your horn!

The sheep's in the meadow, the
cow's in the corn.

Where's the little boy that looks
after the sheep?

Under the haystack, fast asleep.

A treasure to a little boy does not consist of money, gems or jewelry. He will find far greater pleasure in the wonder of a rock, pebble, stick or beetle.

——UNKNOWN

LET THE GOOD TIMES ROLL

If you need a little mother/son or father/son time, here are a few suggestions that your little boy will love!

- Share an ice cream sundae
- Find a new playground
- Read a book
- Snuggle
- Take a class together
- Be silly
- Make a fort
- Go to the movies
- Fly a kite
- Play a sport
- Dance!
- Play a board game
- Take a walk
- Make paper airplanes
- Catch bugs or frogs
- Fix something together
- Make a sand castle
- Bake a treat
- Use your imagination
- Do a craft
- Explore
- Tickle and tackle
- Build
- Sing songs
- Race
- Cook a meal
- Volunteer
- Paint each other's portrait
- Make holiday decorations
- Go on a treasure hunt
- Play a card game
- Do a puzzle
- Visit a friend
- Go see a play
- Play tag
- Make up stories
- Go to the museum
- Have a puppet show
- Paint each other's faces
- Tell knock-knock jokes
- Play hide-and-go-seek
- Go fishing

The Valiant Little Tailor

BY THE BROTHERS GRIMM

ne summer's morning a little tailor was sitting on his table by the window; he was in good spirits, and sewed with all his might. Then came a peasant woman down the street crying: "Good jams, cheap! Good jams, cheap!" This rang pleasantly in the tailor's ears; he stretched his delicate head out of the window, and called: "Come up here, dear woman; here you will get rid of your goods." The woman came up the three steps to the tailor with her heavy basket, and he made her unpack all the pots for him. He inspected each one, lifted it up, put his nose to it, and at length said: "The jam seems to me to be good, so weigh me out four ounces, dear woman, and if it is a quarter of a pound that is of no consequence." The woman who had hoped to find a good sale, gave him what he desired, but went away quite angry and grumbling. "Now, this jam shall be blessed by God," cried the little tailor, "and give me health and strength"; so he brought the bread out of the cupboard, cut himself a piece right across the loaf and spread the jam over it. "This won't taste bitter," said he, "but I will just finish the jacket before I take a bite." He laid the bread near him, sewed on, and in his joy, made bigger and bigger stitches. In the meantime the smell of the sweet jam rose to where the flies were sitting in great numbers, and they were attracted and descended on it in hosts. "Hi! who invited you?" said the little tailor, and drove the unbidden guests away. The flies, however, who understood no German, would not be turned away, but came back again in ever-increasing companies. The little tailor at last lost all patience, and drew a piece of cloth from the hole under his work-table, and saying: "Wait, and I will give it to you," struck it mercilessly on them. When he drew it away and counted, there lay before him no fewer than seven, dead and with legs stretched out. "Are you a fellow of that sort?" said he, and could not help admiring his own bravery. "The whole town shall know of this!" And the little tailor hastened to cut himself a girdle, stitched it, and embroidered on it in large letters: "Seven at one stroke!" "What, the town!" he continued, "the whole world shall hear of it!" and his heart wagged with joy like a lamb's tail. The tailor put on the girdle, and resolved to go forth into the world, because he thought his workshop was too small for his valor. Before he went away, he sought about in the house to see if there was anything which he could take with him; however, he found nothing but an old cheese, and that he put in his pocket. In front of the door he observed a bird which had caught itself in the thicket. It had to go into his pocket with the cheese.

Now he took to the road boldly, and as he was light and nimble, he felt no fatigue. The road led him up a mountain, and when he had reached the highest point of it, there sat a powerful giant looking peacefully about him. The little tailor went bravely up, spoke to him, and said: "Good day, comrade, so you are sitting there overlooking the widespread world! I am just on my way thither, and want to try my luck. Have you any inclination to go with me?" The giant looked contemptuously at the tailor, and said: "You ragamuffin! You miserable creature!"

"Oh, indeed?" answered the little tailor, and unbuttoned his coat, and showed the giant the girdle, "there may you read what kind of a man I am!" The giant read: "Seven at one stroke," and thought that they had been men whom the tailor had killed, and began to feel a little respect for the tiny fellow. Nevertheless, he wished to try him first, and took a stone in his hand and squeezed it together so that water dropped out of it. "Do that likewise," said the giant, "if you have strength." "Is that all?" said the tailor, "that is child's play with us!" and put his hand into his pocket, brought out the soft cheese, and pressed it until the liquid ran out of it. "Faith," said he, "that was a little better, wasn't it?" The giant did not know what to say, and could not believe it of the little man. Then the giant picked up a stone and threw it so high that the eye could scarcely follow it. "Now, little mite of a man, do that likewise," "Well thrown," said the tailor, "but after all the stone came down to earth again; I will throw you one which shall never come back at all," and he put his hand into his pocket, took out the bird, and threw it into the air. The bird, delighted with its liberty, rose, flew away and did not come back. "How does that shot please you, comrade?" asked the tailor. "You can certainly throw," said the giant, "but now we will see if you are able to carry anything properly." He took the little tailor to a mighty oak tree which lay there felled on the ground, and said: "If you are strong enough, help me to carry the tree out of the forest." "Readily," answered the little man; "take you the trunk on your shoulders, and I will raise up the branches and twigs; after all, they are the heaviest." The giant took the trunk on his shoulder, but the tailor seated himself on a branch, and the giant, who could not look round, had to carry away the whole tree, and the little tailor into the bargain: he behind, was quite merry and happy, and whistled the song: "Three tailors rode forth from the gate," as if carrying the tree were child's play. The giant, after he had dragged the heavy burden part of the way, could go no further, and cried: "Hark you, I shall have to let the tree fall!" The tailor sprang nimbly down, seized the tree with both arms as if he had been carrying it, and said to the giant: "You are such a great fellow, and yet cannot even carry the tree!"

They went on together, and as they passed a cherry tree, the giant laid hold of the top of the tree where the ripest fruit was hanging, bent it down, gave it into the tailor's hand, and bade him eat. But the little tailor was much too weak to hold the tree, and when the giant let it go, it sprang back again, and the tailor was tossed into the air with it. When he had fallen down again without injury, the giant said: "What is this? Have you not strength enough to hold the weak twig?" "There is no lack of strength," answered the little tailor. "Do you think that could be anything to a man who has struck down seven at one blow?

I leapt over the tree because the huntsmen are shooting down there in the thicket. Jump as I did, if you can do it." The giant made the attempt but he could not get over the tree, and remained hanging in the branches, so that in this also the tailor kept the upper hand.

The giant said: "If you are such a valiant fellow, come with me into our cavern and spend the night with us." The little tailor was willing, and followed him. When they went into the cave, other giants were sitting there by the fire, and each of them had a roasted sheep in his hand and was eating it. The little tailor looked round and thought: "It is much more spacious here than in my workshop." The giant showed him a bed, and said he was to lie down in it and sleep. The bed, however, was too big for the little tailor; he did not lie down in it, but crept into a corner. When it was midnight, and the giant thought that the little tailor was lying in a sound sleep, he got up, took a great iron bar, cut through the bed with one blow, and thought he had finished off the grasshopper for good. With the earliest dawn the giants went into the forest, and had quite forgotten the little tailor, when all at once he walked up to them quite merrily and boldly. The giants were terrified, they were afraid that he would strike them all dead, and ran away in a great hurry.

The little tailor went onwards, always following his own pointed nose. After he had walked for a long time, he came to the courtyard of a royal palace, and as he felt weary, he lay down on the grass and fell asleep. Whilst he lay there, the people came and inspected him on all sides, and read on his girdle: "Seven at one stroke." "Ah!" said they, "what does the great warrior want here in the midst of peace? He must be a mighty lord." They went and announced him to the king, and gave it as their opinion that if war should break out, this would be a weighty and useful man who ought on no account to be allowed to depart. The counsel pleased the king, and he sent one of his courtiers to the little tailor to offer him military service when he awoke. The ambassador remained standing by the sleeper, waited until he stretched his limbs and opened his eyes, and then conveyed to him this proposal. "For this very reason have I come here," the tailor replied, "I am ready to enter the king's service." He was therefore honorably received, and a special dwelling was assigned him.

The soldiers, however, were set against the little tailor, and wished him a thousand miles away. "What is to be the end of this?" they said among themselves. "If we quarrel with him, and he strikes about him, seven of us will fall at every blow; not one of us can stand against him." They came therefore to a decision, betook themselves in a body to the king, and begged for their dismissal. "We are not prepared," said they, "to stay with a man who kills seven at one stroke." The king was sorry that for the sake of one he should lose all his faithful servants, wished that he had never set eyes on the tailor, and would willingly have been rid of him again. But he did not venture to give him his dismissal, for he dreaded lest he should strike him and all his people dead, and place himself on the royal throne. He thought about it for a long time, and at last found good counsel. He sent to the little tailor and caused him to be informed that as he was a great warrior, he had one request to make to him. In a forest of his country lived two giants, who caused great mischief with their robbing, murdering, ravaging, and burning, and no one could approach them without putting himself in danger of death. If the tailor conquered and killed these two giants, he would give him his only daughter to wife, and half of his kingdom as a dowry, likewise one hundred horsemen should go with him to assist him. "That would indeed be a fine thing for a man like me!" thought the little tailor. "One is not offered a beautiful princess and half a kingdom every day of one's life!" "Oh, yes," he replied, "I will soon subdue the giants, and do not require the help of the hundred horsemen to do it; he who can hit seven with one blow has no need to be afraid of two."

The little tailor went forth, and the hundred horsemen followed him. When he came to the outskirts of the forest, he said to his followers: "Just stay waiting here, I alone will soon finish off the giants." Then he bounded into the forest and looked about right and left. After a while he perceived both giants. They lay sleeping under a tree, and snored so that the branches waved up and down. The little tailor, not idle, gathered two pocketsful of stones, and with these climbed up the tree. When he was halfway up, he slipped down by a branch, until he sat just above the sleepers, and then let one stone after another fall on the breast of one of the giants. For a long time the giant felt nothing, but at last he awoke, pushed his comrade, and said: "Why are you knocking me?" "You must be dreaming," said the other, "I am not knocking you." They laid themselves down to sleep again, and then the tailor threw a stone down on the second. "What is the meaning of this?" cried the other. "Why are you pelting me?" "I am not pelting you," answered the first, growling. They disputed about it for a time, but as they were weary they let the matter rest, and their eyes closed once more. The little tailor began his game again, picked out the biggest stone, and threw it with all his might on the breast of the first giant. "That is too bad!" cried he, and sprang up like a madman, and pushed his companion against the tree until it shook. The other paid him back in the same coin, and they got into such a rage that they tore up trees and belabored each other so long, that at last they both fell down dead on the ground at the same time. Then the little tailor leapt down. "It is a lucky thing," said he, "that they did not tear up the tree on which I was sitting, or I should have had to sprint on to another like a squirrel; but we tailors are nimble."

He drew out his sword and gave each of them a couple of thrusts in the breast, and then went out to the horsemen and said: "The work is done; I have finished both of them off, but it was hard work! They tore up trees in their sore need, and defended themselves with them, but all that is to no purpose when a man like myself comes, who can kill seven at one blow." "But are you not wounded?" asked the horsemen. "You need not concern yourself about that," answered the tailor, "they have not bent one hair of mine." The horsemen would not believe him, and rode into the forest; there they found the giants swimming in their blood, and all round about lay the torn-up trees.

The little tailor demanded of the king the promised reward; he, however, repented of his promise, and again bethought himself how he could get rid of the hero. "Before you receive my daughter, and the half of my kingdom," said he to him, "you must perform one more heroic deed. In the forest roams a unicorn which does great harm, and you must catch it first." "I fear one unicorn still less than two giants. Seven at one blow, is my kind of affair." He took a rope and an ax with him, went forth into the forest, and again bade those who were sent with him to wait outside. He had not long to seek. The unicorn soon came towards him, and rushed directly on the tailor, as if it would gore him with its horn without more ado. "Softly, softly; it can't be done as quickly as that," said he, and stood still and waited until the animal was quite close, and then sprang nimbly behind the tree. The unicorn ran against the tree with all its strength, and stuck its horn so fast in the trunk that it had not the strength enough to draw it out again, and thus it was caught. "Now, I have got the bird," said the tailor, and came out from behind the tree and put the rope round its neck, and then with his ax he hewed the horn out of the tree, and when all was ready he led the beast away and took it to the king.

The king still would not give him the promised reward, and made a third demand. Before the wedding the tailor was to catch him a wild boar that made great havoc in the forest, and the huntsmen should give him their help. "Willingly," said the tailor, "that is child's play!" He did not take the huntsmen with him into the forest, and they were well pleased that he did not, for the wild boar had several times received them in such a manner that they had no inclination to lie in wait for him. When the boar perceived the tailor, it ran on him with foaming mouth and whetted tusks, and was about to throw him to the ground, but the hero fled and sprang into a chapel which was near and up to the window at once, and in one bound out again. The boar ran after him, but the tailor ran round outside and shut the door behind it, and then the raging beast, which was much too heavy and awkward to leap out of the window, was caught. The little tailor called the huntsmen thither that they might see the prisoner with their own eyes. The hero, however, went to the king, who was now, whether he liked it or not, obliged to keep his promise, and gave his daughter and the half of his kingdom. Had he known that it was no warlike hero, but a little tailor who was standing before him, it would have gone to his heart still more than it did. The wedding was held with great magnificence and small joy, and out of a tailor a king was made.

After some time the young queen heard her husband say in his dreams at night: "Boy, make me the doublet, and patch the pantaloons, or else I will rap the yard-measure over your ears." Then she discovered in what state of life the young lord had been born, and next morning complained of her wrongs to her father, and begged him to help her to get rid of her husband, who was nothing else but a tailor. The king comforted her and said: "Leave your bedroom door open this night, and my servants shall stand outside, and when he has fallen asleep shall go in, bind him, and take him on board a ship which shall carry him into the wide world." The woman was satisfied with this; but the king's armor-bearer, who had heard all, was friendly with the young lord, and informed him of the whole plot. "I'll put a screw into that business," said the little tailor. At night he went to bed with his wife at the usual time, and when she thought that he had fallen asleep, she got up, opened the door, and then lay down again. The little tailor, who was only pretending to be asleep, began to cry out in a clear voice: "Boy, make me the doublet and patch me the pantaloons, or I will rap the yard-measure over your ears. I smote seven at one blow. I killed two giants, I brought away one unicorn, and caught a wild boar, and am I to fear those who are standing outside the room." When these men heard the tailor speaking thus, they were overcome by a great dread, and ran as if the wild huntsman were behind them, and none of them would venture anything further against him. So the little tailor was and remained a king to the end of his life.

A small boy, mischievous
to the imp degree.

—REA MURTHA

WHAT'S IN A NAME?

These lists of popular names in decades past provide a unique opportunity to talk about history and tradition with your son. Take time to look back in your family tree and see what names you find!

1920s

- Robert
- John
- James
- William
- Charles
- George
- Joseph
- Richard
- Edward
- Donald

1930s

- Robert
- James
- John
- William
- Richard
- Charles
- Donald
- George
- Thomas
- Joseph

1940s

- James
- Robert
- John
- William
- Richard
- David
- Charles
- Thomas
- Michael
- Ronald

1950s

- James
- Michael
- Robert
- John
- David
- William
- Richard
- Thomas
- Mark
- Charles

1960s

- Michael
- David
- John
- James
- Robert
- Mark
- William
- Richard
- Thomas
- Jeffrey

1970s

- Michael
- Christopher
- Jason
- David
- James
- John
- Robert
- Brian
- William
- Matthew

1980s

- Michael
- Christopher
- Matthew
- Joshua
- David
- James
- Daniel
- Robert
- John
- Joseph

CRAFT TIME
Make Your Own Crayons

What You'll Need:

→ Broken crayon pieces
→ Mini muffin pan
→ Nonstick cooking spray

1. Preheat oven to 275°F. Coat the pan very lightly with nonstick cooking spray.

2. Remove any paper from the old crayons, and break them into small pieces. Fill the muffin tin with the crayon pieces. You can make multicolored crayons, or group similar colors together, whatever you like!

3. Bake the crayons until they have melted, about 7–8 minutes. (Note: When the crayons begin to melt, you can use a toothpick to swirl and blend the colors.)

4. Remove the muffin pan from the oven, let your new crayons cool, and color away!

Jack and the Beanstalk

ACK SELLS THE COW

Once upon a time there was a poor widow who lived in a little cottage with her only son Jack.

Jack was a giddy, thoughtless boy, but very kind-hearted and affectionate. There had been a hard winter, and after it the poor woman had suffered from fever and ague. Jack did no work as yet, and by degrees they grew dreadfully poor. The widow saw that there was no means of keeping Jack and herself from starvation but by selling her cow; so one morning she said to her son, "I am too weak to go myself, Jack, so you must take the cow to market for me, and sell her."

Jack liked going to market to sell the cow very much; but as he was on the way, he met a butcher who had some beautiful beans in his hand. Jack stopped to look at them, and the butcher told the boy that they were of great value, and persuaded the silly lad to sell the cow for these beans.

When he brought them home to his mother instead of the money she expected for her nice cow, she was very vexed and shed many tears, scolding Jack for his folly. He was very sorry, and mother and son went to bed very sadly that night; their last hope seemed gone.

At daybreak Jack rose and went out into the garden.

"At least," he thought, "I will sow the wonderful beans. Mother says that they are just common scarlet-runners, and nothing else; but I may as well sow them."

So he took a piece of stick, and made some holes in the ground, and put in the beans.

That day they had very little dinner, and went sadly to bed, knowing that for the next day there would be none and Jack, unable to sleep from grief and vexation, got up at day-dawn and went out into the garden.

What was his amazement to find that the beans had grown up in the night, and climbed up and up till they covered the high cliff that sheltered the cottage, and disappeared above it! The stalks had twined and twisted themselves together till they formed quite a ladder.

"It would be easy to climb it," thought Jack.

And, having thought of the experiment, he at once resolved to carry it out, for Jack was a good climber. However, after his late mistake about the cow, he thought he had better consult his mother first.

WONDERFUL GROWTH OF THE BEANSTALK

So Jack called his mother, and they both gazed in silent wonder at the Beanstalk, which was not only of great height, but was thick enough to bear Jack's weight.

"I wonder where it ends," said Jack to his mother; "I think I will climb up and see."

His mother wished him not to venture up this strange ladder, but Jack coaxed her to give her consent to the attempt, for he was certain there must be something wonderful in the Beanstalk; so at last she yielded to his wishes.

Jack instantly began to climb, and went up and up on the ladder-like bean till everything he had left behind him—the cottage, the village, and even the tall church tower—looked quite little, and still he could not see the top of the Beanstalk.

Jack felt a little tired, and thought for a moment that he would go back again; but he was a very persevering boy, and he knew that the way to succeed in anything is not to give up. So after resting for a moment he went on.

After climbing higher and higher, till he grew afraid to look down for fear he should be giddy, Jack at last reached the top of the Beanstalk, and found himself in a beautiful country, finely wooded, with beautiful meadows covered with sheep. A crystal stream ran through the pastures; not far from the place where he had got off the Beanstalk stood a fine, strong castle.

Jack wondered very much that he had never heard of or seen this castle before; but when he reflected on the subject, he saw that it was as much separated from the village by the perpendicular rock on which it stood as if it were in another land.

While Jack was standing looking at the castle, a very strange-looking woman came out of the wood, and advanced towards him.

She wore a pointed cap of quilted red satin turned up with ermine, her hair streamed loose over her shoulders, and she walked with a staff. Jack took off his cap and made her a bow.

"If you please, ma'am," said he, "is this your house?"

"No," said the old lady. "Listen, and I will tell you the story of that castle.

"Once upon a time there was a noble knight, who lived in this castle, which is on the borders of Fairyland. He had a fair and beloved wife and several lovely children: and as his neighbors, the little people, were very friendly towards him, they bestowed on him many excellent and precious gifts.

"Rumor whispered of these treasures; and a monstrous giant, who lived at no great distance, and who was a very wicked being, resolved to obtain possession of them.

"So he bribed a false servant to let him inside the castle, when the knight was in bed and asleep, and he killed him as he lay. Then he went to the part of the castle which was the nursery, and also killed all the poor little ones he found there.

"Happily for her, the lady was not to be found. She had gone with her infant son, who was only two or three months old, to visit her old nurse, who lived in the valley; and she had been detained all night there by a storm.

"The next morning, as soon as it was light, one of the servants at the castle, who had managed to escape, came to tell the poor lady of the sad fate of her husband and her pretty babes. She could scarcely believe him at first, and was eager at once to go back and share the fate of her dear ones; but the old nurse, with many tears, besought her to remember that she had still a child, and that it was her duty to preserve her life for the sake of the poor innocent.

`The lady yielded to this reasoning, and consented to remain at her nurse's house as the best place of concealment; for the servant told her that the giant had vowed, if he could find her, he would kill both her and her baby. Years rolled on. The old nurse died, leaving her cottage and the few articles of furniture it contained to her poor lady, who dwelt in it, working as a peasant for her daily bread. Her spinning-wheel and the milk of a cow, which she had purchased with the little money she had with her, sufficed for the scanty subsistence of herself and her little son. There was a nice little garden attached to the cottage, in which they cultivated peas, beans, and cabbages, and the lady was not ashamed to go out at harvest time, and glean in the fields to supply her little son's wants.

"Jack, that poor lady is your mother. This castle was once your father's, and must again be yours."

Jack uttered a cry of surprise.

"My mother! oh, madam, what ought I to do? My poor father! My dear mother!"

"Your duty requires you to win it back for your mother. But the task is a very difficult one, and full of peril, Jack. Have you courage to undertake it?"

"I fear nothing when I am doing right," said Jack.

"Then," said the lady in the red cap, "you are one of those who slay giants. You must get into the castle, and if possible possess yourself of a hen that lays golden eggs, and a harp that talks. Remember, all the giant possesses is really yours." As she ceased speaking, the lady of the red hat suddenly disappeared, and of course Jack knew she was a fairy.

Jack determined at once to attempt the adventure; so he advanced, and blew the horn which hung at the castle portal. The door was opened in a minute or two by a frightful giantess, with one great eye in the middle of her forehead.

As soon as Jack saw her he turned to run away, but she caught him, and dragged him into the castle.

"Ho, ho!" she laughed terribly. "You didn't expect to see me here, that is clear! No, I shan't let you go again. I am weary of my life. I am so overworked, and I don't see why I should not have a page as well as other ladies. And you shall be my boy. You shall clean the knives, and black the boots, and make the fires, and help me generally when the giant is out. When he is at home I must hide you, for he has eaten up all my pages hitherto, and you would be a dainty morsel, my little lad."

While she spoke she dragged Jack right into the castle. The poor boy was very much frightened, as I am sure you and I would have been in his place. But he remembered that fear disgraces a man; so he struggled to be brave and make the best of things.

"I am quite ready to help you, and do all I can to serve you, madam," he said, "only I beg you will be good enough to hide me from your husband, for I should not like to be eaten at all."

"That's a good boy," said the Giantess, nodding her head; "it is lucky for you that you did not scream out when you saw me, as the other boys who have been here did, for if you had done so my husband would have awakened and have eaten you, as he did them, for breakfast. Come here, child; go into my wardrobe: he never ventures to open *that*; you will be safe there."

And she opened a huge wardrobe which stood in the great hall, and shut him into it. But the keyhole was so large that it admitted plenty of air, and he could see everything that took place through it. By-and-by he heard a heavy tramp on the stairs, like the lumbering along of a great cannon, and then a voice like thunder cried out;

"Fe, fa, fi-fo-fum,

I smell the breath of an Englishman.

Let him be alive or let him be dead,

I'll grind his bones to make my bread."

"Wife," cried the Giant, "there is a man in the castle. Let me have him for breakfast."

"You are grown old and stupid," cried the lady in her loud tones. "It is only a nice fresh steak off an elephant, that I have cooked for you, which you smell. There, sit down and make a good breakfast."

And she placed a huge dish before him of savory steaming meat, which greatly pleased him, and made him forget his idea of an Englishman being in the castle. When he had breakfasted he went out for a walk; and then the Giantess opened the door, and made Jack come out to help her. He helped her all day. She fed him well, and when evening came put him back in the wardrobe.

THE HEN THAT LAYS GOLDEN EGGS

The Giant came in to supper. Jack watched him through the keyhole, and was amazed to see him pick a wolf's bone, and put half a fowl at a time into his capacious mouth.

When the supper was ended he bade his wife bring him his hen that laid the golden eggs.

"It lays as well as it did when it belonged to that paltry knight," he said; "indeed I think the eggs are heavier than ever."

The Giantess went away, and soon returned with a little brown hen, which she placed on the table before her husband. "And now, my dear," she said, "I am going for a walk, if you don't want me any longer."

"Go," said the Giant; "I shall be glad to have a nap by-and-by."

Then he took up the brown hen and said to her:

"Lay!" And she instantly laid a golden egg.

"Lay!" said the Giant again. And she laid another.

"Lay!" he repeated the third time. And again a golden egg lay on the table.

Now Jack was sure this hen was that of which the fairy had spoken.

By-and-by the Giant put the hen down on the floor, and soon after went fast asleep, snoring so loud that it sounded like thunder.

Directly Jack perceived that the Giant was fast asleep, he pushed open the door of the wardrobe and crept out; very softly he stole across the room, and, picking up the hen, made haste to quit the apartment. He knew the way to the kitchen, the door of which he found was left ajar; he opened it, shut and locked it after him, and flew back to the Beanstalk, which he descended as fast as his feet would move.

When his mother saw him enter the house she wept for joy, for she had feared that the fairies had carried him away, or that the Giant had found him. But Jack put the brown hen down before her, and told her how he had been in the Giant's castle, and all his adventures. She was very glad to see the hen, which would make them rich once more.

THE MONEY BAGS

Jack made another journey up the Beanstalk to the Giant's castle one day while his mother had gone to market; but first he dyed his hair and disguised himself. The old woman did not know him again, and dragged him in as she had done before, to help her to do the work; but she heard her husband coming, and hid him in the wardrobe, not thinking that it was the same boy who had stolen the hen. She bade him stay quite still there, or the Giant would eat him.

Then the Giant came in saying:

"Fe, fa, fi-fo-fum,

I smell the breath of an Englishman.

Let him be alive or let him be dead,

I'll grind his bones to make my bread."

"Nonsense!" said the wife, "it is only a roasted bullock that I thought would be a tit-bit for your supper; sit down and I will bring it up at once." The Giant sat down, and soon his wife brought up a roasted bullock on a large dish, and they began their supper. Jack was amazed to see them pick the bones of the bullock as if it had been a lark. As soon as they had finished their meal, the Giantess rose and said:

"Now, my dear, with your leave I am going up to my room to finish the story I am reading. If you want me call for me."

"First," answered the Giant, "bring me my money bags, that I may count my golden pieces before I sleep." The Giantess obeyed. She went and soon returned with two large bags over her shoulders, which she put down by her husband.

"There," she said; "that is all that is left of the knight's money. When you have spent it you must go and take another baron's castle."

"That he shan't, if I can help it," thought Jack.

The Giant, when his wife was gone, took out heaps and heaps of golden pieces, and counted them, and put them in piles, till he was tired of the amusement. Then he swept them all back into their bags, and leaning back in his chair fell fast asleep, snoring so loud that no other sound was audible.

Jack stole softly out of the wardrobe, and taking up the bags of money (which were his very own, because the Giant had stolen them from his father), he ran off, and with great difficulty descending the

Beanstalk, laid the bags of gold on his mother's table. She had just returned from town, and was crying at not finding Jack.

"There, mother, I have brought you the gold that my father lost."

"Oh, Jack! you are a very good boy, but I wish you would not risk your precious life in the Giant's castle. Tell me how you came to go there again."

And Jack told her all about it.

Jack's mother was very glad to get the money, but she did not like him to run any risk for her.

But after a time Jack made up his mind to go again to the Giant's castle.

THE TALKING HARP

So he climbed the Beanstalk once more, and blew the horn at the Giant's gate. The Giantess soon opened the door; she was very stupid, and did not know him again, but she stopped a minute before she took him in. She feared another robbery; but Jack's fresh face looked so innocent that she could not resist him, and so she bade him come in, and again hid him away in the wardrobe.

By-and-by the Giant came home, and as soon as he had crossed the threshold he roared out:

"Fe, fa, fi-fo-fum,

I smell the breath of an Englishman.

Let him be alive or let him be dead,

I'll grind his bones to make my bread."

"You stupid old Giant," said his wife, "you only smell a nice sheep, which I have grilled for your dinner."

And the Giant sat down, and his wife brought up a whole sheep for his dinner. When he had eaten it all up, he said:

"Now bring me my harp, and I will have a little music while you take your walk."

The Giantess obeyed, and returned with a beautiful harp. The framework was all sparkling with diamonds and rubies, and the strings were all of gold.

"This is one of the nicest things I took from the knight," said the Giant. "I am very fond of music, and my harp is a faithful servant."

So he drew the harp towards him, and said:

"Play!"

And the harp played a very soft, sad air.

"Play something merrier!" said the Giant.

And the harp played a merry tune.

"Now play me a lullaby," roared the Giant; and the harp played a sweet lullaby, to the sound of which its master fell asleep.

Then Jack stole softly out of the wardrobe, and went into the huge kitchen to see if the Giantess had gone out; he found no one there, so he went to the door and opened it softly, for he thought he could not do so with the harp in his hand.

Then he entered the Giant's room and seized the harp and ran away with it; but as he jumped over the threshold the harp called out:

"Master! Master!"

And the Giant woke up.

With a tremendous roar he sprang from his seat, and in two strides had reached the door.

But Jack was very nimble. He fled like lightning with the harp, talking to it as he went (for he saw it was a fairy), and telling it he was the son of its old master, the knight.

Still the Giant came on so fast that he was quite close to poor Jack, and had stretched out his great hand to catch him. But, luckily, just at that moment he stepped upon a loose stone, stumbled, and fell flat on the ground, where he lay at his full length.

This accident gave Jack time to get on the Beanstalk and hasten down it; but just as he reached their own garden he beheld the Giant descending after him.

"Mother O Mother!" cried Jack, "make haste and give me the ax."

His mother ran to him with a hatchet in her hand, and Jack with one tremendous blow cut through all the Beanstalks except one.

"Now, mother, stand out of the way!" said he.

THE GIANT BREAKS HIS NECK

Jack's mother shrank back, and it was well she did so, for just as the Giant took hold of the last branch of the Beanstalk, Jack cut the stem quite through and darted from the spot.

Down came the Giant with a terrible crash, and as he fell on his head, he broke his neck, and lay dead at the feet of the woman he had so much injured.

Before Jack and his mother had recovered from their alarm and agitation, a beautiful lady stood before them.

"Jack," said she, "you have acted like a brave knight's son, and deserve to have your inheritance restored to you. Dig a grave and bury the Giant, and then go and kill the Giantess."

"But," said Jack, "I could not kill anyone unless I were fighting with him; and I could not draw my sword upon a woman. Moreover, the Giantess was very kind to me."

The Fairy smiled on Jack.

"I am very much pleased with your generous feeling," she said. "Nevertheless, return to the castle, and act as you will find needful."

Jack asked the Fairy if she would show him the way to the castle, as the Beanstalk was now down. She told him that she would drive him there in her chariot, which was drawn by two peacocks. Jack thanked her, and sat down in the chariot with her.

The Fairy drove him a long distance round, till they reached a village which lay at the bottom of the hill. Here they found a number of miserable-looking men assembled. The Fairy stopped her carriage and addressed them:

"My friends," said she, "the cruel giant who oppressed you and ate up all your flocks and herds is dead, and this young gentleman was the means of your being delivered from him, and is the son of your kind old master, the knight."

The men gave a loud cheer at these words, and pressed forward to say that they would serve Jack as faithfully as they had served his father. The Fairy bade them follow her to the castle, and they marched thither in a body, and Jack blew the horn and demanded admittance.

The old Giantess saw them coming from the turret loop-hole. She was very much frightened, for she guessed that something had happened to her husband; and as she came downstairs very fast she caught her foot in her dress, and fell from the top to the bottom and broke her neck.

When the people outside found that the door was not opened to them, they took crowbars and forced the portal. Nobody was to be seen, but on leaving the hall they found the body of the Giantess at the foot of the stairs.

Thus Jack took possession of the castle. The Fairy went and brought his mother to him, with the hen and the harp. He had the Giantess buried, and endeavored as much as lay in his power to do right to those whom the Giant had robbed.

Before her departure for fairyland, the Fairy explained to Jack that she had sent the butcher to meet him with the beans, in order to try what sort of lad he was.

"If you had looked at the gigantic Beanstalk and only stupidly wondered about it," she said, "I should have left you where misfortune had placed you, only restoring her cow to your mother. But you showed an inquiring mind, and great courage and enterprise, therefore you deserve to rise; and when you mounted the Beanstalk you climbed the Ladder of Fortune."

She then took her leave of Jack and his mother.

CRAFT TIME
Make Your Own Face Paint

What You'll Need:

➻ 1 teaspoon cornstarch
➻ ½ teaspoon cold cream
➻ ½ teaspoon cold water
➻ Food coloring

1. Mix cornstarch, cold cream, and cold water together well so there are no lumps. If the consistency is too thin, add more cornstarch; if it's too thick, add a little more water.

2. Divide the mixture into different bowls or cups. Add food coloring to make as many colors as you desire.

3. You can use more of the cold cream to remove the face paint when you're finished!

REFERENCE PAGE

The Other Pages. "According to Ambrose" by Stephen L. Spanoudis. *www.theotherpages .org/quote-14.html*. Accessed 14 June 2011.

Sheldon Vanauken, *A Severe Mercy* (New York: Harper Collins, 1980).

Rousseau, Jean-Jacques. *Émile, or On Education*. Trans. Allan Bloom. (New York: Basic books, 1979), 37.

Aesop. *Aesop's Fables. www.gutenberg.org/ebooks/28.* Accessed 2 June 2011.

Andersen, Hans Christian. *Hans Andersen's Fairy Tales: First Series. www.gutenberg .org/ebooks/32571.* Accessed 1 June 2011.

Audet, Marye. *The Everything Cookies & Brownies Cookbook*. (Avon, MA: Adams Media, 2009).

Fact Monster. "20th-Century Toys and Games Timeline." Last updated May 01, 2011. *www .factmonster.com/ipka/A0768872.html.*

Fuess, Claude Moore and Harold Crawford Stearns. *The Little Book of Society Verse. www.bartleby .com/263/115.html.* Accessed 3 June 2011.

Grimm, Jacob and Wilhelm. *Grimms' Fairy Tales. www.gutenberg.org/ebooks/2591.* Accessed 2 June 2011.

Grover, Eulalie Osgood. *Mother Goose: The Original Volland Edition. www.gutenberg .org/ebooks/24623.* Accessed 2 June 2011.

The Holy Bible, King James Version. (New York: American Bible Society, 1999); Bartleby. com, 2000. *www.bartleby.com/108/.* Accessed 11 May 2011.

How Stuff Works. "23 Must-Have Toys from the 1950s and Beyond" by the Editors of Publications International, Ltd., *http://entertainment.howstuffworks.com/23-must-have-toys-from-the-1950s-and-beyond.htm.* Accessed 19 March 2011.

Lang, Andrew. *The Blue Fairy Book. www.gutenberg.org/ebooks/503.* Accessed 31 May 2011.

Lang, Andrew. *The Crimson Fairy Book. www.gutenberg.org/ebooks/2435.* Accessed 3 June 2011.

Lang, Andrew. *The Red Fairy Book. www.gutenberg.org/ebooks/540.* Accessed 3 June 2011.

Opie, I. and P. *The Oxford Dictionary of Nursery Rhymes.* 2nd edition. (Oxford, UK: Oxford University Press, 1997).

Perrault, Charles. *The Fairy Tales of Charles Perrault. www.gutenberg.org/ebooks/29021.* Accessed 2 June 2011.

Quiller-Couch, Arthur (ed). *The Oxford Book of Verse 1250-1900. www.bartleby.com/101/513.html.* Accessed 3 June 2011.

Roberts, Dan. "The Best Selling Toys of the Last 50 Years." *www.dad.info/entertainment/books-toys-and-games/the-best-selling-toys-of-the-last-50-years.* Accessed 19 March 2011.

Social Security Administration. "Popular Baby Names by Decade." Last modified May 14, 2010. Social Security Online, *www.ssa.gov/oact/babynames/decades/index.html.*

Stevenson, Robert Louis. *A Child's Garden of Verses. www.gutenberg.org/ebooks/136.* Accessed 2 June 2011.

Toys Timeline, KPaul Media, *www.toystimeline.com.* Accessed 19 March 2011.

Various. *Aunt Kitty's Stories. www.gutenberg.org/ebooks/24760.* Accessed 2 June 2011.

Wright, Blanche Fisher. *Real Mother Goose. www.gutenberg.org/ebooks/10607.* Accessed 31 May 2011.

About the Author

M. L. Stratton is a freelance editor who has been working in the publishing industry for over eight years. From editing presentations for worldwide IT conferences, to creating pamphlets for small non-profits, to blogging about her life at home, much of her world is wrapped up in words. On the off chance she's not chasing her three energetic kids around, you'll probably find her armed either with a book and a cup of tea, or a paintbrush and a pickaxe, working with her husband David to fix up her 163-year-old Cape.

When You Don't Have Time for Anything Else

Visit our Cereal for Supper blog and join other over-inundated, under-celebrated, multi-tasking moms for an (almost) daily allowance of parenting advice—and absolution.

You won't learn how to make handmade Martha Stewart–inspired hankie holders or elaborate gourmet dinners—but you will find heaping spoonfuls of support and a few laughs along the way!

Sign up for our newsletter now at
www.adamsmedia.com/blog/parenting
And get our FREE Top Ten Recipes for Picky Eaters!